Richard C. Foltz

ANIMALS IN ISLAMIC TRADITION AND MUSLIM CULTURES

Related titles from Oneworld

Richard C. Foltz

ANIMALS IN ISLAMIC TRADITION AND MUSLIM CULTURES

ONEWORLD

OXFORD

ANIMALS IN ISLAMIC TRADITION AND MUSLIM CULTURES

Oneworld Publications
(Sales and Editorial)
185 Banbury Road
Oxford OX2 7AR
England
www.oneworld-publications.com

ISBN-13: 978–1–85168–397–0 (hardback)
ISBN-10: 1–85168–397–6 (hardback)
ISBN-13: 978–1–85168–398–7 (paperback)
ISBN-10: 1–85168–398–4 (paperback)

Cover design by Mungo Designs
Typeset by Jayvee, Trivandrum, India
Printed and bound in India by Thomson Press Ltd.

To Bijan

CONTENTS

PREFACE

This is a book I had hoped someone else would write. I have long felt that such a book is much needed, above all as a resource for Muslims. Islamic communities, however, have well-known and established criteria for determining who has authority to speak for the tradition, and I do not meet those criteria. I have not studied at any recognized institution of traditional Islamic learning; I have not received an *ijāza* (permission to teach) from any acknowledged authority on Islamic law. A Ph.D. from an American university does not carry much weight in traditional Muslim circles when it comes to religious questions, nor perhaps should it.

To my mind, at least, it would have been preferable for this book to have been written by, say, a practicing *'ālim* (religious scholar) with a large following, or perhaps a law professor at the University of Jiddah, so that its credibility would be harder to assail. Or alternatively, had the arguments it contains been put forth by one of the Muslim world's great contemporary radical thinkers, such as Khaled Abou El-Fadl, Farid Esack, or Abdol-Karim Soroush, it might have hoped to stir up debate within Muslim communities, at least among intellectuals. Perhaps one day they will be taken up, but for now it seems that all of these brilliant minds are too preoccupied with the many crises currently facing the human animal alone to focus very much on other species or our relations with them. I have tried myself to persuade some of these eminent figures to devote a little time and thought to inter-species questions, and failed.

So I am not sure that what I have to offer here will be seen as having much value for Muslims, though I will be most pleasantly surprised if it is. I suspect, however, that the audience for this book is more likely to be non-Muslims who are sympathetic to Muslim culture and interested in learning more about what it has to offer in terms of animal rights. I hope that this audience too will not be disappointed in what they find here, for this book is not an exercise in apologetics. The Islamic tradition does indeed offer much that can lend itself to respect for species other than our own, but it also contains much that is problematic from an animal rights activist point of view. And even much of what could resemble animal rights within the tradition is unheeded by most Muslims or unknown to them.

Having made clear my own lack of confidence and trepidation in writing this book, I cannot fault readers for asking why I have written it. The answer is simple enough: because there needs and deserves to be something available on the subject of animals in Islam, and for the present at least, no one else seemed prepared to do it.* In the Persian language, one of the commonest expressions heard in daily conversation is *ghorbān-e shomā*, "May I be a sacrifice for you" (literally, "I am your sacrificial animal"). Such is the spirit of humility which, hopefully, underlies this book.

I am grateful to Paul Waldau, whose invitation spurred me to write my first short survey of Islam and animals, to Martin Rowe, for encouraging me to expand that survey to a book-length treatment, and to Ayatollah Hasan Emami of Esfahan for kindly providing me with a copy of Jazayery's book on animals in (Shi'i) Islam. I am indebted to Richard Bulliet, Chris Chapple, Khalid Keshk, and Robert Tappan for their comments on the typescript and, as always, to Désirée and Shahrzad who are my dearest

---

* To be fair, there do exist several short treatments, listed in the bibliography, but apart from the fact that all have serious weaknesses (not the least of which is an unwillingness to examine the tradition critically), they are mostly out of print and extremely hard to find.

friends in the world. Novin Doostdar and the staff at Oneworld have been a continuing source of support and encouragement. Finally, I would like to thank my dog, Max, one of the strangest and at times most difficult of the many non-humans I have lived with, but also the most loving, forgiving, and non-judgmental, for constantly reminding and teaching me that human needs are no more pressing, important, or real than non-human ones, and indeed often less so.

INTRODUCTION: ISLAM, MUSLIMS, AND NON-HUMAN ANIMALS

Discussions about the presence and roles of non-human animals in world religions have only recently come to be a part of academic inquiry, despite the fact that every religious tradition is full of stories about non-human animals and how humans interact with them. Paul Waldau cautions us, however, that "Although such accounts can be surpassingly beautiful, they also can be positively misleading about the realities of other animals."[1]

Religions are our primary source for codes of ethics, but these ethical systems are often considered to apply only to how we treat members of our own species. The international animal rights movement, which has its roots in early nineteenth-century England but really only began to flourish after the publication of moral philosopher Peter Singer's book *Animal Liberation* in 1975, has demonstrated the arbitrariness – and, ultimately, the indefensibility – of ethical systems that draw a boundary at the species barrier.[2] Unfortunately religions, and cultures generally, have been slow to pick up on the logic-based arguments provided by philosophy, so while in certain areas there has been real change in our treatment of non-human animals, it has fallen far short of what a genuinely just and compassionate ethics would require. In general it would seem that "speciesism" – which Singer likens to racism and sexism, and defines as "a prejudice or attitude of bias toward the interests of members of one's own species and against those of members of other species" – remains the dominant paradigm in human societies all over the world.[3]

Perhaps the main issue to arise in re-considering our ethics toward non-human animals is whether or not we can justify eating them, and the means by which we prepare them to be eaten. If we do choose to accord animals rights, certainly the most fundamental of these is the right to live. Thus, the vegetarian option must be engaged by anyone genuinely seeking to extend moral considerability to non-human animals. Some religions, especially in South Asia, have engaged this issue for thousands of years, while others (notably the Semitic traditions) have positively refused to do so.

But the use of animals for food is only one dimension of inter-species ethics. Historically, humans have used other animals as work slaves, as companions, and as objects for violent sport. Today, issues such as scientific experimentation and habitat destruction have been added to the mix. In none of these domains has the level of critical discourse in any mainstream human society kept pace with the realities of our treatment of other species.

The Islamic religion, while being the focus of much attention these days, does not often come up in discussions on animal rights. If the connection can be made at all, for many non-Muslims the most visible expression of how Muslims view animals may be the 'Īd al-Adha, the Feast of Sacrifice, which from the point of view of millions of domestic animals can only appear as an annually recurring global holocaust. The popular Muslim aversion to dogs and pigs, as well as the Arab affinity for camels and horses, are all well-known stereotypes. But to suppose that these isolated tendencies are representative of Muslim attitudes toward animals in general would be a narrow view indeed.

It should not be imagined that religious traditions will automatically determine an individual's attitudes toward other living species (or, indeed, toward any issue), or that a simple reinterpretation of religion will lead the tradition's adherents to change their attitudes and behaviors. However, it may be argued that, for a believer, it will be difficult (though perhaps not impossible) to adopt a position which appears to be in contradiction to the teachings of one's tradition. Likewise, there exists at least the possibility that, for the devout, an argument based on the sources of religious tradition will be more convincing than one that is not.

This is nowhere more true than within the world's Muslim communities today, where much effort is expended toward addressing an overwhelming diversity of cultural norms by appealing to those particular normative sources – usually texts – which can be argued to be universally "Islamic." This is not to say that attitudes and practices which turn out to be unique to a particular Muslim community are incontestably "extra-Islamic" (though they may well be), but only that they may have little appeal for Muslims who do not share that localized source of cultural norms.

Thus, while attempting to identify "the mainstream" in any human context is undeniably problematic, in this book "mainstream Islam" will be understood as having its basis in the Sunni legal tradition. This choice is in no way intended to marginalize the millions of Muslims who do not see Sunni law as their primary normative source; it is merely a practical concession to the reality that the overwhelming majority of the world's Muslims – at least 80 percent – identify themselves as Sunnis, and among that population the legal tradition is more widely con-sidered acceptable than any other basis of common values.

For Muslims, "universal" sources such as the Qur'an, the *hadith*s (reports about the words and deeds of the Prophet Muhammad), the *shari'a* (Islamic law), as well as the non-universal sources of popular tradition, all speak of non-human animals, which are treated as more or less omnipresent figures in the lives of humans and thus have a whole range of familiar relationships with them. Less is said about wild animals than about domestic species, who are obviously more familiar and with whom a greater proportion of humans interact on a daily basis.

In all these various expressions of Muslim culture, non-human animals are valued mainly for the services they provide for humans, though sometimes it is for the lessons which humans can draw from them. Even insects have instructive value, as the Qur'an itself indicates in a chapter called "The Bee."[4] A popular story from Abbasid times has the Caliph ask the greatest jurist of the period, Muhammad ibn Idris al-Shafi'i, why God created such annoying creatures as flies, to which the scholar replies, "In my humble opinion the purpose is to show those in power their own helplessness."[5]

Indeed the Islamic tradition, perhaps more so than any other, has much to say about the need to respect all parts of God's creation, even insects. Numerous passages in the Qur'an indicate a sensitivity to the fact that animals have interests and value of their own, entirely apart from their usefulness to humans; the hadiths and the legal tradition show this as well. But whatever teachings Islam may have to offer on the subject of human relations with non-human animal species, it is worth pointing out that people are usually only partially aware of what is taught by their own inherited tradition, and are often highly selective about those aspects that are known to them.

It would be misleading, then, to assume that just because one can find certain guidelines or injunctions regarding the treatment of non-human animals in Islamic texts, all or most Muslims in the world must therefore abide by them, for such is not the case. As with the laws and morals of any society, Islamic norms are often flouted, distorted, or simply ignored. More confusing still, individual Muslims will often claim that a particular view or practice is "Islamic" even if it derives not from the religious tradition *per se* but rather from their own particular local culture. Therefore, while any sort of generalization is likely to be problematic, on balance it would probably be safe to say that Muslims as a whole are no more and no less animal-friendly than humans of other cultures, regardless of the many distinctive teachings about animals that exist within the tradition.

Muslims are not prominent participants in animal rights discussions today, but that may be at least partly due to the fact that much of the Muslim world is so beset by all manner of injustices between humans that it is hard to look beyond the concerns of our own species. It is perhaps natural to have little outrage left over for the abuse of livestock, the torture of laboratory specimens, or the extinction of species, when so much is consumed by the murder of civilians, the denial of democratic process, and the deprivation of basic human rights, the sources of which are both external and internal to Muslim societies. Natural perhaps, but not entirely acceptable, because there is nothing in Islam which states that rights cease at the species boundary.

It may be said that animal rights awareness is not entirely absent in the Muslim world either, even if it is very much overshadowed by other concerns. In better times, historically, non-human animals in Muslim societies benefited from protections and services that filled European visitors with astonishment. Already in the sixteenth century French essayist Michel de Montaigne noted that "The Turks have alms and hospitals for animals."[6] These institutions, which were funded through religious endowments (*waqfs*), would have appeared to most Europeans of the time as a frivolous waste of public resources.

In the nineteenth century, English traveler Edward Lane remarked that the Egyptians seemed to be losing some of their traditional kindness towards animals, but wrote that he was "... inclined to think that the conduct of Europeans has greatly conduced to produce this effect, for I do not remember to have seen acts of cruelty to dumb animals except in places where Franks [that is, Europeans] either reside or are frequent visitors ..."[7]

Taking the long view of history, an average non-human animal might well have preferred to live among Muslims than among Christians. Christian theology has been particularly hard on non-human animals, even if a few lonely theological voices (Andrew Linzey, Jay McDaniel) have lately begun to call for revisions. While a handful of progressive churches – the cathedral St. John the Divine in New York City, for example – now offer animal masses and animal blessings, none yet approaches the inclusiveness of the Islamic tradition which states that unlike humans, *all* non-human animals are believers; that humans, in fact, are the *only* species with a cosmic problem!

This difference is not lost on Muslims today. I have an Iranian friend who teaches at a small college in rural upstate New York. People often ask him whether he is sometimes uncomfortable being the only Muslim in the vicinity. "What do you mean?" he tells them with a grand sweep of his hand, "Just look at all these cows!"

So if all non-human animals are "Muslims," and not all humans are, does that mean that it is better to be a non-human animal? The crucial difference, at least according to mainstream Islam, is that humans alone possess *taqwa* (consciousness), which implies that we alone can be judged for our acts. While this accountability presents risks to humans that non-human animals do not face, it also holds out the prospect of eternal life in paradise. Most Muslims do not believe that non-human animals have an afterlife, although the view has at times been debated.

For example, according to a hadith related by Abu Hurayra,

On the Day of Arising, all of creation will be gathered together: the cattle, the riding-beasts, the birds, and every other thing, and it shall be God's justice (Exalted is He!) that He takes the hornless sheep's case against the horned one. Then he shall say, "Be dust!" which is the time at which the unbeliever says, "Would that I were dust!"[8]

Non-human animals, in other words, will be extinguished on the Day of Judgment, a fate that non-Muslim humans, destined for eternal hell-fire, will envy.

Mainstream Islam posits that non-human animals have souls, even if they are not eternal. This can be favorably contrasted with the Christian position, which states categorically (though arbitrarily and without evidence) that souls belong to humans alone. The Muslim philosophers, however, like the ancient Greeks, did differentiate between the "animal soul" and the "rational soul," asserting that the latter is possessed only by humans. Better an animal soul, perhaps, than none at all . . .

On the other hand, according to some of the Mu'tazilites (a radical school of Islamic theologians who became prominent in the early ninth century), good animals, like good humans, will enjoy eternal life in heaven, while bad animals will join bad humans in hell. One Mu'tazilite theologian, Abu Ishaq al-Nazzam (a teacher of the famous Arab writer Abi Uthman Amr ibn Badr al-Jahiz), even claimed that *all* animals would go to heaven, although this was refuted by al-Baghdadi who retorted that "He is very welcome to a heaven which contains pigs, dogs and snakes."[9]

On the whole, then, it would seem that among Muslims, as in any human culture, attitudes towards animals vary greatly and, indeed, encompass all possibilities, from animal-loving revisionists to hardcore anthropocentrists. To single out any one view as uniquely authoritative or normative would be to take a partisan stand, and would not do justice to the rich diversity of ideas that has always been present in one of the world's great religious traditions and the many cultures which inform it.

The point of this book, in any case, is not to demonstrate whether Islam and Muslims are more or less animal-friendly than other religions and their practitioners. Each cultural community has its own history and its own norms, and deserves to be assessed first and foremost according to its own standards and claims about itself. But cultures have always learned from each other as well, and this is a good thing – even, one might say in today's interconnected world, indispensable.

It is difficult to deny that the modern West has produced the most egregious forms of institutionalized violence against animals the world has ever seen: factory farming, laboratory testing, habitat depletion – the list goes on. But the West has also, from Jeremy Bentham and Henry Salt up through Peter Singer and Carol Adams, generated the most sophisticated critiques of the kind of unexamined anthropocentrism that has made such crimes appear morally acceptable. Other cultures have, unfortunately, learned to replicate many of the callous attitudes and cruel forms of abuse pioneered in the West. On the other hand, they may yet prove willing to investigate and integrate some of the West's critical responses as well, in concert with those generated from within the value systems of their own communities.

In the Muslim world, such a discourse has barely begun. And yet, as this book aims to show, the Islamic tradition possesses ample resources by which to develop and apply a meaningful contemporary critique of how humans today treat other animals, if and when significant numbers of Muslims should decide to do so.

Muslims and Islam: Some Facts and Definitions

Muslims, as the practitioners of the religion called Islam are known, currently number more than 1.2 billion, and are dispersed throughout virtually every country on earth. Contrary to certain popular notions which remain prevalent, the vast majority – about 85 percent – are not Arab but belong to other ethnic and linguistic groups. In fact the world's largest concentration of Muslims is to be found not in the Middle East (25 percent), but in South Asia (33 percent). The nations with the largest Muslim populations are Indonesia, India, Bangla Desh, and Pakistan. Since Muslim identities and worldviews are in all cases comprised of multiple sources, one might predict that attitudes toward non-human animals among Muslims of diverse cultural backgrounds would show both similarities and differences, as indeed turns out to be the case.

Though claims are frequently made that one position or another represents "true" Islam, the notion should be dispelled that there exists a unified "Islamic" or "Muslim" view of non-human animals. A related point is that these are not identical terms, since attitudes held by individuals or collectives who happen to be Muslim may or may not be "Islamic."[10] Disentangling the two is often difficult, both for those within and outside the tradition, but it is important to acknowledge that the two adjectives, "Muslim" and "Islamic," are not synonymous.

Islam (literally, "submission"), as an ideal distinct from real-life Muslims who aspire in varying degrees to practice it, is understood by believers as the state God (Allah) wills for His creation (*khalq*). This is apprehended by the Sunni majority through the revealed scripture of the Qur'an, the life example of the Prophet Muhammad (the *sunna*, as attested in hadith reports), and the *shari'a*, a comprehensive code of life as articulated in the legal texts of the so-called Classical period (eighth to tenth centuries CE). Shi'ites also follow the teachings of their infallible Imams, and Sufi mystics (who can be Sunni or Shi'i) defer to the authority of their spiritual guides (*shaykh*s, or *pīr*s).

The actual practices and attitudes of Muslims have always been shaped by Islamic sources in combination with extra-Islamic cultural ones. Islamic sources tend to be embodied in authoritative texts, while cultural sources often are not. This book will attempt to survey the references to non-human animals in both specifically "Islamic" and broadly "Muslim" contexts.

1

ANIMALS IN ISLAMIC SOURCE TEXTS

Islam is a text-bound religion, perhaps more so than any other. Muslims believe that the one true god, Allah, revealed His divine will in its definitive form to an Arab prophet, Muhammad of Mecca (ca. 570–632 CE), over the last twenty-three years of the Prophet's life. This body of revelation is known as the Qur'an, and forms the basis of Islamic belief. Six of the Qur'an's 114 chapters (called *sūra*s) are named for animals: the Cow (*sūra* 2), the Cattle (*sūra* 6), the Bee (*sūra* 16), the Ant (*sūra* 28), the Spider (*sūra* 29), and the Elephant (*sūra* 105). Among the animal species mentioned by name in the Qur'an one may find camels, cattle, horses, mules, donkeys, sheep, monkeys, dogs, pigs, snakes, worms, ants, bees, spiders, mosquitoes, and flies.

Much of Islam's textual tradition is originally in Arabic, which for many centuries played the role of scholarly *lingua franca* analogous to that of Latin in Christian Europe. The Arabic word used in the Classical texts to refer to animals, including humans, is *hayawān*.[1] This term appears only once in the Qur'an, however, where it refers rather to the "true" existence of the afterlife.[2] For non-human animals, the Qur'an instead uses the term *dābba* (pl. *dawābb*), which is often translated as "beasts,"[3] or *an'ām* when referring to livestock.[4] Yet another term, *anām* (not to be confused with *an'ām*), carries the more general sense of "living beings," including humans (indeed, Arabic-speakers often understand the term as meaning humans alone, but the Qur'anic sense is arguably more inclusive).[5] The Qur'an states that all animals were created by Allah,[6] "from water,"[7] and in pairs.[8]

Human beings are often described in Arabic texts as "the speaking animal" (*al-hayawān al-nātiq*), despite the fact that the Qur'an itself acknowledges that non-human animals also have speech:

> And [in this insight] Solomon was [truly] David's heir; and he would say: "O you people! We have been taught the speech of birds, and have been given [in abundance] of all [good] things: this, behold, is indeed a manifest favor [from God]!"[9]

And likewise in the following verse:

> At length, when they came to the valley of the ants, one of the ants said, "O ye ants, get into your habitations, lest Solomon and his hosts crush you [underfoot] without knowing it."[10]

The Qur'an occasionally blurs the line between human and non-human animals, suggesting that it is possible for humans to be "demoted" to other species. One verse, for example, refers to "Those whom Allah has cursed, against whom He has been angry, of whom He has made monkeys and pigs because they worshipped the powers of evil."[11] Another verse refers to the Israelites of Moses' time who broke the Sabbath, to whom Allah declared, "Be despicable monkeys!"[12] While it might be possible to read into these verses a metaphorical interpretation, Muslim commentaries have tended to take them literally.

The Role of Arab Norms

Though most Muslims today are not Arabs (and, for that matter, millions of Arabs are not Muslims), the Qur'an was revealed in an

Arab context to an Arab prophet. Inevitably, therefore, Arab culture played a huge role in the formative years of the tradition.
While the Qur'an "corrected" certain aspects of Arab practice –
abolishing female infanticide, for example, and extending legal
rights to women – any prevailing practice or norm not specifically
addressed in the Qur'an was assumed by the first Arab Muslims
to be acceptable. Since Islam was initially brought to neighboring
societies by Arabs, such norms carried the weight of the dominant
class and were often absorbed by the conquered peoples.

Arabs in pre-Islamic times practiced animal cults, various
meat taboos, sympathetic magic (*istimtar*) and possibly totemism.
Some tribes had animal names, such as the Quraysh ("shark"),
which was the tribe of the Prophet Muhammad, the Kalb ("dog"),
and the Asad ("lion").[13] Certain animals, including camels,
horses, bees, and others, were believed to carry blessing (*baraka*),
while others, such as dogs and cats, were associated with the
evil eye. Genies (*jinn*) were believed sometimes to take animal
form. As in many cultures, pre-Islamic Arabs associated particular
animals with human traits, such as the lion with bravery, the
rooster with generosity, and the buzzard with stupidity.

The most important animal to the pre-Islamic Arabs was
without question the camel, a species which provided them with
food, shelter, clothing, and transportation. Due to its high value,
the camel was considered the greatest sacrificial offering and was
slaughtered at the time of the pilgrimage, to welcome honored
guests, and often on the death of its owner (so as to serve him in
the afterlife). The Bedouin believed that eating camel-flesh was a
religious act of devotion, and that the appearance of camels in
dreams was an auspicious sign.[14]

The Qur'an proscribed certain pre-Islamic practices related
to animals, such as the consecration of animals to specific
deities. For example, according to contemporary commentator
Muhammad Asad, the verse, "It is not of God's ordaining that
certain kinds of cattle should be marked out by superstition and
set aside from the use of man,"[15] refers to "certain categories of
domestic animals which the pre-Islamic Arabs used to dedicate to
their various deities by setting them free to pasture and prohibiting

their use or slaughter."[16] The Qur'an clarifies that pre-Islamic taboos on the eating of cattle did not originate with Allah and should be abandoned, and, in passing, indicates that the Islamic requirement that an animal be slaughtered while pronouncing Allah's name had pre-Islamic origins.[17]

The Arabs had many kinds of blood sacrifices, which mostly survived into the Islamic period though often in altered form. The most visible of the Islamic blood sacrifices, which is performed once a year by all Muslims able to afford it, is the Feast of Sacrifice ('Īd al-Adha), commemorating the prophet Abraham's willingness to sacrifice his son (Isma'il, not Isaac, in Islamic tradition). Many Muslims also make blood sacrifices in fulfillment of vows (*nazr*), seven days after the birth of a child (*aqīqa*), or on the tenth day of the lunar month of Dhu'l-hijja in atonement for transgressions committed during the pilgrimage to Mecca (*ḥājj*). The proper method for sacrificing an animal is called _ḏhabh_ in Islamic law, the sacrificial victim being known as a _ḏhabīha_.

The only aspect of _ḏhabh_ mentioned in the Qur'an is the saying of Allah's name at the time of sacrifice;[18] the remainder comes from hadiths and the Islamic legal tradition. In answer to the question of why Muslims were allowed to continue animal sacrifice, Muhammad is reported as having said, "This is a tradition (*sunna*) of your patriarch Abraham."[19] Thus, the Qur'an itself does not specifically *require* Muslims to sacrifice animals, for food or for any other reason; it merely *permits* them to do so. And even then, the Qur'an reminds Muslims that if they do sacrifice animals, "neither their flesh nor their blood reaches Allah; it is only your righteousness that reaches Him."[20]

A belief in metamorphosis (*maskh*) also survived from pre-Islamic times, several examples occurring in the Qur'an.[21] Some heterodox Muslim groups even retained a belief in metempsychosis (*tanasukh*), but mainstream Islam considers such ideas to be heresy. Among the pre-Islamic Arab traditions that the Prophet Muhammad forbade to his followers, we find the practice of animal fights (though camel fighting remained popular, especially in Muslim India) and the cutting off of camel-humps and sheep-tails for food while leaving the animal alive.[22]

Cosmic Hierarchy in the Qur'an

Islam is what contemporary animal rights activists would probably call a strongly anthropocentric religion, although Muslims
themselves might prefer to see their worldview as "theocentric."
Within the hierarchy of Creation, the Qur'an depicts humans
as occupying a special and privileged status. The Qur'an says,
"Certainly, we have created Man in the best make,"[23] and "Hast
thou not seen how Allah has subjected (*sakhkhara*) to you all that
is in the earth?"[24] The term *khalīfa* (lit., "successor"), which in
the Qur'an is applied to humans, is generally defined by contemporary Muslims as "vice-regent," as in the verses that state "I am
setting on the earth a vice-regent (*khalīfa*)," and "It is He who
has made you his vice-regent on earth."[25]

According to this view, while non-human Creation is subju-
gated to human needs, the proper human role is that of conscientious steward and not exploiter.[26] "To Allah belong all things in
the heavens and on earth"[27] – that is to say, *not* to humans. Moreover, the earth was not created for the sake of humans alone:
"And the earth has He spread out for all living beings (*anām*)."[28]
The Qur'an emphasizes that God takes care of the needs of all
living things: "There is no moving creature on earth, but Allah
provides for its sustenance."[29] Everything in Creation is a miraculous sign of God (*āya*), inviting Muslims to contemplate the
Creator. Non-human animals are explicitly included among
God's miraculous signs, both in general ". . . The beasts of all
kinds that He scatters throughout the earth . . ."[30] and in terms of
specific species, as in the following verse:

> . . . This she-camel of God is a sign to you; so leave her to
> graze in God's earth, and let her come to no harm, or you
> shall be seized with a grievous punishment.[31]

And the following:

> Do they not look at the birds, held poised in the middle of
> [the air and] the sky? Nothing holds them up but [the
> power of] Allah. Verily in this are signs for those who
> believe.[32]

The "divine sign" can also be a negative lesson:

> The parable of those who take protectors other than Allah is
> that of the spider, who builds [for itself] a house; but truly the
> flimsiest of houses is the spider's house, if they but knew.[33]

Nevertheless, the Qur'an specifies that certain animals were
created for the benefit of humans:

> And He has created cattle for you: you derive warmth from
> them, and [various] other uses; and from them you obtain
> food; and you find beauty in them when you drive them
> home in the evenings and when you take them out to pas-
> ture in the mornings. And they carry your loads to [many]
> a place which [otherwise] you would be unable to reach
> without great hardship to yourselves. And [it is He who
> creates] horses and mules and asses for you to ride, as well
> as for [their] beauty: and He will yet create things of which
> [today] you have no knowledge.[34]

And

> Of the cattle some are for carrying and some for food; eat
> what Allah hath provided for you, and follow not the foot-
> steps of Satan for he is to you an avowed enemy.[35]

In fact, the Qur'anic "correction" of the pre-Islamic Arab practice of leaving certain "sacred" cattle unmolested[36] can be interpreted to mean that it is against God's will for humans *not* to use
domestic animals for the purposes mentioned in the divine revelation. Just letting them be, it would seem, is not an option.

It is not only domestic creatures that are created for utilitarian
ends. Marine animals, too, are said to exist so as to serve as food
for humans:

> It is He who has made the sea subject, that you may eat the
> flesh thereof that is fresh and tender.[37]

Yet despite the clear inter-species hierarchy established in the
Qur'an, humans are described as similar to non-human animals
in almost all respects. The Qur'an states in several places that all

creation praises God, even if this praise is not expressed in human language.[38] In a verse which constitutes the very core of Islamic teaching on animal rights, the Qur'an further says that "There is not an animal (*dābba*) in the earth, nor a flying creature on two wings, but they are communities (*umam*, sg. *umma*) like you."[39]

A jurist from the Classical period, Ahmad ibn Habit, even surmised from this verse that since the Qur'an elsewhere states that "there never was a community (*umma*) without a warner [that is, a prophet] having lived among them,"[40] then perhaps non-human animals also have prophets. Ibn Hazm (d. 1062) denied this, arguing that "the laws of Allah are only applicable to those who possess the ability to speak and can understand them,"[41] but his rebuttal lacks weight since the Qur'an explicitly states that animals do speak, albeit in their own languages.

Non-human animals can even receive divine revelation, as in the verse which states: "And your Lord revealed to the bee, saying: 'make hives in the mountains, and in the trees, and in [human] habitations.'"[42] It has thus been argued by some Islamic commentators that humans are unique only in that they possess volition (*taqwa*), and are thus responsible for their actions.[43]

The Hadiths

Authority in Islam has no real parallel in Western tradition. There is no pope, no governing council, no universally acknowledged source of normative values – except, in a general sense, the Qur'an itself. But relying solely on the Divine Revelation as a source of guidance presents numerous practical problems for Muslims. For one thing, it is in Arabic, a language most Muslims don't understand, and moreover, its style is a lofty seventh-century variety that most Arabs even at the time probably didn't fully grasp. Mastering Qur'anic Arabic takes a lifetime of study; thus, in reality, the content of the Qur'an reaches most Muslims in a mediated form through the scholarly elite.

Furthermore, the Qur'an is not a lengthy text – particularly in comparison with the sacred works of other religious traditions – and much if not most of what humans have to deal with in their everyday lives is not addressed in it explicitly. (Whether the Qur'an speaks more broadly on an esoteric level is a question that highlights both the need for interpretation and the inevitability of disagreement.) So very early on, beginning in the eighth century, Muslim scholars began to collect and compare accounts of the words and deeds of the Prophet Muhammad as a supplementary basis for guidance, relying on the Qur'anic assurance that "You had a beautiful model (*uswa hasana*) in the Messenger of God."[44]

The collecting of such accounts, the hadiths, took many decades and resulted in an almost unfathomable quantity of material, much of which many Muslims suspected to be spurious. The Classical authors of hadith collections, of which there are many, therefore ranked individual accounts as "sound," "good," "weak," or "spurious." Among the many hadith collections produced in the eighth and ninth centuries, Sunni Muslims came to accept two as being the best, the "Sound" (*Sahīh*) collections of Bukhari (d. 870) and Muslim (d. 875), and four more – the *Traditions* (*Sunān*) of Ibn Maja (d. 886), Abu Dawud (d. 889), Tirmidhi (d. 892), and Nisa'i (d. 915) – as also trustworthy.[45] Many other collections, such as the *Transmissions* (*Musnad*) of Ahmad Ibn Hanbal and the *Muwatta'* of Malik ibn Anas, exist as well, and Muslims cite them when appropriate.

Shi'ite Muslims – who are the majority in Iran, Iraq and Bahrain and form strong communities in Lebanon, Pakistan, and elsewhere – have their own collections of hadiths, the most important of which is *The Complete* (*Al-Kāfī*) by Abu Ja'far Muhammad al-Kulayni (d. ca. 940).[46] In addition to reports about the words and deeds of the Prophet Muhammad, Shi'ites also consider those of the Imams (descendents of the Prophet who are considered to be the just and infallible leaders of the community) as authoritative. The sayings of Muhammad's nephew and son-in-law, 'Ali, whom Shi'ites consider to be the first Imam, are collected in a work known as *The Pinnacle of Eloquence* (*Nahj al-balāgha*).[47]

Because of the sheer volume of available hadiths, it is possible to argue a prophetic basis for almost any position, and while the ranking of a given hadith can give it more weight in settling an argument, Muslims are not absolutely bound to accept any hadith and some even go so far as to reject all of them.

Many hadiths report Muhammad as reminding his companions to take the interests of non-human animals into consideration. The message of the following hadith seems to be that compassion for animals provides Muslims with an opportunity to gain heavenly recompense:

> Yahya related to me from Malik from Sumayy, the *mawla* (client) of Abu Bakr from Abu Salih al-Samman from Abu Hurayra that the Messenger of Allah, may Allah bless him and grant him peace, said, "A man was walking on a road when he became very thirsty. He found a well and went into it and drank and came out. There was a dog panting and eating earth out of thirst. The man said, 'This dog has become as thirsty as I was.' He went down into the well and filled his shoe and then held it in his mouth until he climbed out and gave the dog water to drink. Allah thanked him for it and forgave him [for his sins]."
>
> They said, "Messenger of Allah, do we have a reward for taking care of beasts?" He said, "There is a reward for [compassion shown to] every one with a moist liver [that is, for every living thing]."[48]

Another hadith, which exists in many versions, reports Muhammad as saying, "There is none amongst the Muslims who plants a tree or sows seeds, and then a bird, or a person or an animal eats from it, but is regarded as a charitable gift for him."[49]

Muhammad enjoined his followers to use animals only for necessary purposes, on one occasion reprimanding some men who were sitting idly on their camels in the marketplace, saying "Do not treat the backs of your animals as pulpits, for God Most High has made them subject to you only to convey you to a place which you could not otherwise have reached without much difficulty."[50]

When traveling, Muhammad encouraged his followers to ride slowly if there was vegetation, so that their animals could graze,

and quickly when in the desert; at night, they were to be protected from insects.[51] Acts of cruelty such as branding or hitting
an animal in the face were forbidden.[52]

Muhammad seems to have recognized that animals have an
emotional life which needs to be respected. Once a Companion of
the Prophet was showing off some bird's eggs he had found, while
the mother bird fluttered about frantically. The Prophet is
reported to have said, "Who has caused this bird distress by
taking the eggs from her nest? Return them to her."[53] In another
instance, Muhammad spoke against the cutting of a horse's fore-
lock, noting that "it is in the horse's seemliness or decorum."[54] He
once upbraided his favorite wife, 'Aisha, for being rough with her
camel, telling her "It behooves you to treat the animals gently."[55]

Regarding wild animals, Muhammad forbade hunting for
sport.[56] Wild animal skins were not to be used as rugs or saddle
covers,[57] although the skins of domestic animals can be used for
these purposes (presumably since they have already been killed
for a "legitimate" purpose, namely as food). Muhammad is also
reported to have said, "There is no man who kills [even] a spar-
row or anything smaller, without its deserving it, but Allah will
question him about it [on the Day of Judgment]."[58] Similarly,
while in the hadith mentioned earlier God forgives a sinner for
showing compassion for a thirsty dog, in another hadith a
woman is condemned to hell for torturing a cat.[59]

The hadiths portray the Prophet as having insisted on the protection of some animal species while calling for others to be killed
(though generally only when they pose some specific danger to
humans or human interests). Muhammad disallowed the killing
of frogs, because he believed their croaking was in praise of Allah.
Likewise he forbade Muslims to kill magpies, because they were
said to have been the first to perform the fast. Ants and bees were
to be preserved as they were mentioned as the recipients of divine
revelation. One well-known hadith has God reprimanding one of
His prophets for needlessly destroying an ant colony:

Abu Huraira reported Allah's Messenger (may peace be
upon him) as saying: "An ant had bitten a Prophet (one

amongst the earlier Prophets) and he ordered that the colony of the ants should be burnt. And Allah revealed to him: 'Because of an ant's bite you have burnt a community from amongst the communities which sings My glory.' "⁶⁰

Other animals which Muslims are never to kill include hoopoes, swallows, and bats. On the other hand, Muhammad ordered the killing of mottled crows, dogs, mice, poisonous snakes, and scorpions. He permitted his followers to kill certain animals – including rats and mice, scorpions, crows, kites, wild dogs, lions, leopards, lynxes and wolves – even when in a state of ritual purity (*ihram*) during pilgrimage.⁶¹ Muhammad is also reported as having commanded that in cases of bestiality, both perpetrator and victim were to be killed:

> The Prophet (peace be upon him) said: If anyone has sexual intercourse with an animal, kill him and kill it along with him. I (Ikrimah) said: I asked him (Ibn Abbas): What offence can be attributed to the animal? He replied: I think he (the Prophet) disapproved of its flesh being eaten when such a thing had been done to it.⁶²

Interestingly, the following entry reports that the Prophet never prescribed punishment for bestiality. The apparent inconsistency between the two reports illustrates the ambiguity often present in hadith accounts.

Shi'ite hadith collections differ considerably from those used by Sunnis in that Shi'ites admit different chains of transmitters, and because they include reports not only of the Prophet but also of his successors the Imams, they are more extensive. Moreover, because many of the Imams lived and traveled outside Arabia, the contexts for Shi'ite hadith stories are more varied than in the case of Sunni hadiths, though many hadiths are also accepted by both sects (albeit through different transmitters).

One notable feature found in Shi'ite hadith accounts is that Muhammad and the Imams are portrayed as being able to converse with animals. Animals are sometimes reported as speaking in Sunni hadiths as well, but this is rare and presented in a less direct and matter-of-fact way as in Shi'ite stories. To give an example from the Sunni hadiths:

> The Prophet said, "While a man was riding a cow, it turned towards him and said, 'I have not been created for this purpose (that is, carrying), I have been created for sloughing.'" The Prophet added, "I, Abu Bakr and 'Umar believe in the story." The Prophet went on, "A wolf caught a sheep, and when the shepherd chased it, the wolf said, 'Who will be its guard on the day of wild beasts, when there will be no shepherd for it except me?'" After narrating it, the Prophet said, "I, Abu Bakr and 'Umar too believe it." Abu Salama said, "Abu Bakr and 'Umar were not present then."

It has been written that a wolf also spoke to one of the companions of the Prophet near Medina as narrated in Fatah-al-Bari:

> Narrated Unais bin 'Amr: Ahban bin Aus said, "I was amongst my sheep. Suddenly a wolf caught a sheep and I shouted at it. The wolf sat on its tail and addressed me, saying, 'Who will look after it (that is, the sheep) when you will be busy and not able to look after it? Do you forbid me the provision which Allah has provided me?'" Ahban added, "I clapped my hands and said, 'By Allah, I have never seen anything more curious and wonderful than this!' On that the wolf said, 'There is something (more curious) and wonderful than this; that is, Allah's Apostle in those palm trees, inviting people to Allah (that is, Islam).'" Unais bin 'Amr further said, "Then Ahban went to Allah's Apostle and informed him what happened and embraced Islam."[63]

While such passages are unusual in the context of Sunni hadiths, numerous Shi'ite accounts have the Prophet or his descendants conversing nonchalantly with camels, birds, and other species, listening to their complaints and responding to them with compassion and understanding.[64] The following hadith is typical:

> One day the Holy Prophet (Peace be Upon Him) was sitting somewhere when a camel came up and kneeled down

beside him, and began to lament, complaining to the Holy Prophet (Peace be Upon Him) in its own language. The Holy Prophet (Peace be Upon Him) asked, "Who is the owner of this camel?" He was told that such-and-such was the camel's owner. The Holy Prophet (Peace be Upon Him) said, "Bring him to me." So the camel's owner came to the Holy Prophet (Peace be Upon Him). His Excellency told him, "Your camel said, 'I've been working for all of them great and small and have always been at their service, but now they want to kill me.'"

The camel's owner explained, "O Messenger of God, we have the knife ready and wish to sacrifice him." The Holy Prophet (Peace be Upon Him) replied, "For my sake, spare him and don't sacrifice him." The camel's owner immediately offered him to the Holy Prophet (Peace be Upon Him), who set the camel free. The camel then went round to the homes of the Ansar [the Helpers of Medina], who fed him his fill, saying "This must be the camel which the Messenger of God (Peace be Upon Him) set free." And in this way the camel was looked after and cared for.[65]

Similarly, in the following story, the fourth Shi'ite Imam, Zayn al-'Abidin (658–713) shows compassion to a hungry deer while on a picnic with his companions:

One day His Excellency Imam Sajjad (Zayn al-'Abidin), Peace be Upon Him, had gone out to a garden accompanied by some friends. The food arrived and His Excellency ordered it to be spread out. No sooner had the group begun to eat, than a deer came up alongside Imam Sajjad, Peace be Upon Him, and began conversing with the Imam. The group asked His Excellency what the deer had spoken to him about. His Excellency replied that the deer had complained to him of hunger, saying it was three days since he had eaten.

Then, Imam Sajjad, Peace be Upon Him, told the group, "Don't do anything to this deer; because I would like to invite him to eat with us." The group all gave their word not to bother or molest the deer, and to allow it to eat freely until it was full.

Imam Sajjad, Peace be Upon Him, motioned to the deer and invited it to eat. The animal then came and began eating. At this time one man from the group got up and grabbed the deer around the waist; because of this, the deer took fright and ran away from the group. Imam Sajjad, Peace be Upon Him, turned to the group and said, "Didn't you promise me you were going to leave this deer alone?" The man who had put his arm around the deer and was the cause of its fleeing swore that he hadn't meant any harm and didn't intend to frighten the deer.

His Excellency Imam Sajjad, Peace be Upon Him, then spoke to the deer and invited it once again to come and eat, and promised the deer that there was nothing to be afraid of and that nobody from the group would bother it. So the deer returned once again and began eating until it had had its fill. Once it was full, the deer spoke to Imam Sajjad, Peace be Upon Him, in its own language, and then left the group.

The group asked His Excellency Imam Sajjad, Peace be Upon Him, what the deer had said to him. His Excellency Imam Sajjad, Peace be Upon Him, replied, "This deer has prayed for your well-being."[66]

In a similar hadith, a pregnant lion asks Imam Musa al-Kazim to pray for her easy delivery. He does so, and in exchange, the lioness prays for the Imam, as well as for "his children, his partisans (literally, "shi'ites"), and his friends."[67]

Though the theme of compassion toward animals as a sign of piety is a familiar one, these stories emphasize several points more strongly than is found in the Qur'an or the Sunni hadiths. First, the attribution of language to non-human animals is very pronounced. Second, the Imams – like the Prophet himself, but unlike ordinary humans – are able to speak animal languages.

Third, and perhaps most important, animals pray, and their prayers are to be valued.

In the Shiʻite hadiths, at least, animals pray not only for the well-being of good humans, but also call down God's wrath on bad ones, as in a hadith attributed to the eighth Imam, Reza, who warned his followers not to eat the lark or allow children to taunt it, for this species of bird prays repeatedly to God to curse the enemies of the Prophet's family.[68] The Prophet is reported to have enjoined respect for the rooster, whose crowing signals the time for morning prayer; elsewhere, he suggests that the rooster's crowing is its form of prayer.[69]

Meat-eating and Slaughter

Islamic dietary laws as extrapolated in the legal tradition are based on the Qur'an and the hadiths. The overwhelming majority of Muslims eat meat; indeed, meat-eating is mentioned in the Qur'an as one of the pleasures of heaven.[70] The Qur'an appears to allow the eating of animal flesh, with certain exceptions:

> O you who have attained to faith! Be true to your covenants! Lawful to you is every beast that feeds on plants, save what is mentioned to you [hereinafter]: but you are not allowed to hunt while you are in a state of pilgrimage. Behold, God ordains in accordance with his will.[71]

On the other hand the Qur'an prohibits the eating of animals that have not been ritually slaughtered, as well as the eating of blood, and pigs:

> Forbidden to you is carrion, and blood, and the flesh of swine, and that over which any name other than God's has been invoked, and the animal that has been strangled, or beaten to death, or killed by a fall, or gored to death, or savaged by a beast of prey, save that which you [yourselves] may have slaughtered while it was still alive; and [forbidden to you] is all that has been slaughtered on idolatrous altars.[72]

A similar verse, however, adds an exemption in case of dire need:

> ... but if one is driven [to it] by necessity – neither coveting
> it nor exceeding his immediate need – verily, God is much-
> forgiving, a dispenser of grace.[73]

The pre-Islamic Arabs, who often had difficulty finding water
while traveling in the desert, sometimes in desperation would
slaughter a camel and drink its blood. While the Qur'an prohibits
this, the above verse was sometimes invoked to justify the practice as a last resort.

Ritual slaughter (*dhabh*) is said to follow the principle of compassion for the animal being killed. According to a hadith,

> Shaddid ibn Aws said: Two are the things which I remem-
> ber Allah's Messenger (may peace be upon him) having
> said: "Verily Allah has enjoined goodness to everything; so
> when you kill, kill in a good way and when you slaughter,
> slaughter in a good way. So every one of you should
> sharpen his knife, and let the slaughtered animal die
> comfortably."[74]

Yet, on another occasion, when Muhammad saw a man sharpening his knife while an animal waited nearby, he reprimanded him,
"Do you wish to slaughter this animal twice, once by sharpening
your blade in front of it and another time by cutting its throat?"[75]

Ritual sacrifice, such as that customarily performed by Muslims on the occasion of 'Id al-Adha, is not prescribed as a duty in
the Qur'an, but a hadith is sometimes cited to provide the sense
that it is an obligation:

> He who can afford (sacrifice) but he does not offer it, he
> should not come near our places of worship. On the day of
> sacrifice no-one does a deed more pleasing to Allah than
> the shedding of blood of a sacrificed animal who will come
> on the Day of Resurrection with its horns, its hair, its hoofs,
> and will make the scales of his action heavy, and verily its
> blood reaches acceptance of Allah before it falls upon the
> ground; therefore be joyful for sacrificing animals.[76]

As will be seen in chapter six, the question of whether or not Muslims are obligated to perform a blood sacrifice during 'Īd al-Adha has recently become a matter of debate.

In conclusion, from this survey of animal-related material from the main scriptural sources of Islam several points can be drawn. First, the tradition takes the relationship between humans and other animal species quite seriously. Second, animals are seen as having feelings and interests of their own. And third, the overriding ethos enjoined upon humans is one of compassionate consideration.

Based on these sources it would seem that the Islamic ethical system extends moral considerability to non-human animals, although not on the same level as humans. This nevertheless contrasts favorably with the Christian tradition, which has until quite recently had very little to say about the rights or importance of non-human animals, and even more so with the dominant attitudes of the Western Enlightenment which saw non-human animals as nothing more than soulless machines whose sole function was to serve human needs.

2

ANIMALS IN
ISLAMIC LAW

Hadith accounts are the principal source for Islamic law as developed during the eighth through the tenth centuries, alongside the Qur'an, and supplemented by analogical reasoning (*qiyās*) and consensus among scholars (*ijma'*). The corpus of jurisprudence (*fiqh*) derived during this, the so-called Classical period, has come down to us through the canons of four schools of law accepted by Sunni Muslims, who represent about 80 percent of the total world Muslim population. Shi'ites follow a fifth school, based on their own hadith collections and the sayings of their Imams. The schools accepted by Sunnis are those founded by Abu Hanifa (d. 767), Malik ibn Anas (d. 795), Muhammad ibn Idris al-Shafi' (d. 820), and Ahmad ibn Hanbal (d. 855). The Shi'ite school of law is considered to have been founded by the sixth Shi'ite Imam, Ja'far al-Sadiq (d. 765).

The bodies of law formulated by those following the lines of these founding jurists are referred to by Muslims as the *shari'a*, an Arabic term which originally referred to the path a camel takes to reach a water source, but came to be understood as the guidelines laid down by God for every aspect of daily life. The spirit of *shari'a* law is one of acknowledgement, concession, and restraint. That is, it begins from the premise that there are certain things that humans are naturally going to do, and it is important to lay down the conditions under which they can do them. Things that humans are not permitted to do at all constitute a relatively small category.

For example, it is taken as a given that human appetites for possessions, food, sex, and so forth, are natural and acceptable, but that to allow them free rein in seeking to satisfy these appetites would lead to unacceptable levels of social disorder. Two important underlying principles are that 1) people should not be burdened by excessive restrictions, and 2) that anything is lawful unless specifically forbidden. A basis for these principles is found in the following Qur'anic verse:

> O believers! Make not unlawful the good things which Allah has made lawful for you, and exceed not the limits (*la ta'tadū*), for Allah loves not those who overpass limits.[1]

The same general spirit underlies discussion of animals and how to treat them according to *shari'a* law. It is assumed without question that humans are going to make use of animals and to eat them; the legal questions therefore center on how to define and circumscribe the limits of these behaviors. The issues are *which* animals to eat, *how* to kill them properly in preparation for eating, and, to a lesser extent, *what responsibilities* humans have to the animals which serve them. Questions about *whether* humans have the innate right to do these things do not arise.

As has been previously noted, there is no central authority in Islam (apart from, in a general sense, the Qur'an itself), so individual Muslims may follow any of a range of recognized schools of interpretation and guidance. What this means, in terms of authority, is that the average Muslim tends to defer to the judgments of whichever living legal scholar s/he most respects, usually himself a follower of the particular school of law dominant in the region where he lives.[2] Islamic legal scholars have thus enjoyed a privileged position within their communities as consultants on every issue imaginable. This role is often a lucrative one as well, since scholars are paid fees for offering their opinions (*fatwa*s) – which, by the way, contrary to the impression often given in the Western press, are non-binding.

The interesting thing about this system of dispersed authority is that individual Muslims, like modern medical patients, are free to get as many "expert" opinions as they like, and these opinions often differ. So when it comes to animal rights (as with any subject in fact), it is actually possible to envision almost the complete range of opinions on any given question, all claiming to be "Islamic." Nevertheless, over time certain interpretations have come to be accepted as mainstream, while the rest have become marginalized. Still, marginal views can hold on to their claims of being genuinely Islamic, as long as they remain based on the generally accepted sources of law mentioned above.

Animals in the Classical Legal Texts

The traditional law books are typically organized according to topic, including such important religious domains as prayer, fasting, pilgrimage, and the paying of the alms tax (*zakāt*), but also mundane categories such as marriage, business transactions, the freeing of slaves, and so on. Laws pertaining to animals are included under categories such as their treatment, their sale, how to include them in *zakāt* calculations, their lawfulness as food, prescriptions for slaughter, and restrictions on hunting. Thus, animals are discussed both in terms of their use by humans and, less extensively, in terms of the obligations humans have toward them.

In many cases there is little or no difference between the legal interpretations of the various schools of law. When differences are found, they are mostly on matters of fine detail. As an example of the kind of disagreements that occurred among legal scholars in the Classical period, one may cite the question of whether a Muslim may eat the meat of an animal slaughtered by a Jew or a Christian who has not recited the name of God over it. The Hanafi school holds that such meat is not lawful for Muslims. The Shafi'i, Maliki and Hanbali schools, meanwhile, contend that it is, unless the butcher has recited the name of any deity other than Allah over the slaughtered animal.

A broader range of disagreement can be seen in addressing the problem of whether meat is lawful over which a Muslim butcher has neglected to say "God is great" ("*Allahu akbar*"). The Shafi'is say that such meat is undesirable but lawful. The Hanafis opine that the meat is lawful if the butcher merely forgot to recite the formula, while the Malikis say that it is unlawful even if the omission was unintentional.

LAWS PERTAINING TO ANIMALS AS FOOD

The various schools of law each classified all known animals in terms of whether eating them was *halāl* (permissible), *harām* (forbidden), or *makrūh* (discouraged). All schools placed the vast majority of animals in the first, permitted category. Some animals presented special cases; frogs, for example, which would normally meet the conditions for a *halāl* designation, were determined to be *harām* on the basis of a hadith in which Muhammad forbade the eating of frogs.

Differences among the schools regarding these classifications occur mainly in cases of reasoning by analogy, such as whether or not to forbid the eating of animals that have similar names to those of forbidden animals, for example "dogfish." Another kind of ambiguity arises when an animal that would normally be considered *halāl*, such as an eel (which is a kind of fish) resembles an animal which is *harām* (for example, the snake, to which eels appear similar). The Maliki and Shafi'i schools allow the eating of fish found floating dead in the water, while other schools forbid it. Various schools disagree over the lawfulness of eating crustaceans and insects. Carnivores, which are *harām*, are identified in the legal tradition by their possession of fangs or claws; thus, there is disagreement over the lawfulness of eating elephants, since, while herbivores, their tusks resemble fangs.

OBLIGATIONS OF HUMANS TOWARDS ANIMALS

In a general sense one could say that the mainstream Islamic legal tradition accords more rights to non-human animals than do the legal systems of the contemporary West, while still falling short of what animal rights activists might call for. In Islamic law humans do have certain explicit obligations towards animals, whereas in Western tradition laws involving animals have generally referred back to the rights of the animals' human owners.

There is a subtle, if rarely explored, undertone in Islamic law that killing in general is essentially a bad thing. Muslims are not allowed to kill any living thing while in a state of ritual purity (*ihrām*), for example while praying or on pilgrimage. This would seem to indicate that killing itself is seen as an impure act, to be avoided if possible, though such a sweeping connection has rarely been drawn by Muslims.

Nevertheless, the underlying principle seems to be that Muslims should kill animals only to satisfy their hunger or to protect themselves from danger. Even a strictly literal interpretation of the most unambiguous Islamic restrictions on killing, if universally observed, would make for much better treatment of non-human animals than is often the case, whether in Muslim societies or elsewhere.

Wild Animals

On the basis of numerous hadiths, sport hunting, animal baiting, and the killing of wild animals for uses other than food (such as for decorative purposes) are "always" prohibited, though this prohibition has often been ignored in the history of Muslim societies. This has been especially true among ruling elites, for whom hunting has always been a favored pastime and a demonstration of class privilege.

On the other hand, as mentioned in chapter one, some hadiths also call for the killing of certain animals. Some Islamic jurists have argued that these hadiths refer to specific instances and are not meant to serve as general guidelines, but others apply them in the broadest sense. Further, some schools extend these directives through the juristic principle of analogy (*qiyās*), so that the hadiths referring to mice are understood to cover all rodents (except, for some reason, the jerboa).

As a general rule, Islamic law seems to suggest that wild animals should be allowed to live their lives unmolested, provided they do not pose a threat to humans. Birds should be allowed to fly free and not kept in cages as pets.

Domestic Animals

The Shafiʻi jurist ʻIzz al-din ibn ʻAbd al-salam al-Sulami (d. 1262), in his legal treatise *Rules for Judgment in the Cases of Living Beings (Qawāʼid al-ahkām fī masālih al-anām)*, has the following to say about a person's obligations toward his domestic animals:

- He should spend [time, money or effort] on it, even if the animal is aged or diseased in such a way that no benefit is expected from it. His spending should be equal to that on a similar animal useful to him.
- He should not overburden it.
- He should not place with it anything that might cause it harm, whether of the same kind or a different species.
- He should kill it properly and with consideration; he should not cut its skin or bones until its body has become cold and its life has passed fully away.
- He should not kill an animal's young within its sight.
- He should give his animals different resting shelters and watering places, which should all be cleaned regularly.
- He should put the male and female in the same place during their mating season.
- He should not hunt a wild animal with a tool that breaks bones, which would render it unlawful for eating.[3]

The contemporary Shiʻite jurist Hashem Najy Jazayery provides the following variant list of animal rights, based on Shiʻite hadiths:

- Do not brand an animal on the face, and do not hit an animal on the face, because animals pray and praise God Almighty.
- Do not force an animal to carry a load greater than it is able to bear.
- Do not force an animal to travel further than it is able.
- Do not stand on the back, waist, or neck of an animal.
- Do not use your animals' backs as a pulpit.
- Before filling your own belly, think about filling the belly of your animal and give it food.

- Before slaking your own thirst, think of the thirst of your animal and take care of it.
- When taming an animal, do not hit it unnecessarily.
- When an animal is unruly, punish it only to the degree necessary.[4]

Special note may be taken of the fact that in Islamic law the category of water rights extends to animals through the principle of "the right to drink" (*haqq al-shurb*). A Qur'anic basis for this can be found in the verse, "It is the she-camel of Allah, so let her drink!"[5] A non-Muslim American writer has noted with some irony that Islamic law accords non-human animals greater access to water than do the "modern" laws of the United States.[6]

Nevertheless, when it comes to determining compensation for wrongs, the Islamic jurists are clear that, as in Western law, a wrong committed against an animal is really seen as a wrong committed against its owner. Al-Shafi'i, in his *Treatise on the Foundations of Jurisprudence* (*Al-Risāla fī usūl al-fiqh*), has little to say about animals but does include a long debate over whether the compensation for a wrongly killed slave should be calculated in the same way as for a wrongly killed camel.[7]

In any case, while the rights of non-human animals are guaranteed in the legal tradition, their interests are ultimately subordinate to those of humans. According to al-Sulami:

> The unbeliever who prohibits the slaughtering of an animal [for no reason but] to achieve the interest of the animal is incorrect because in so doing he gives preference to a lower, *khasīs*, animal over a higher, *nafīs*, animal.[8]

The medieval jurist seems to have been suggesting that it is actually un-Islamic to argue against killing animals for reasons of compassion. In a similar spirit, Abu Nasr ibn Abi Imran, a leading theologian of the eleventh-century, ridiculed the poet Abu'l-'Ala al-Ma'arri, an ethical vegan, whom he accused of "trying to be more compassionate than God."[9]

Many contemporary animal rights activists would label such positions as "speciesist." If interpretations such as those of the medieval theologians are representative of mainstream Muslim attitudes, it would seem that despite the rights accorded to non-human animals under Islamic law, the tradition not only condones attitudes which could be considered "speciesist," it actually requires them!

The Basis for Wildlife Conservation in Islamic Law

Contemporary Iraqi–British jurist Mawil Izzi Dien, commenting on al-Sulami's statement above, notes that had the medieval jurist been alive today

> he would have had to consider the question of priority due to species extinction. It is crucial to ask: when a certain species of animal is endangered, what represents the imminent harm to the public good? Are we allowed to eat such an endangered animal or are we not? Would it be *harām* to consume it even if it has been ritually slaughtered? The same question applies not only to eating the animal, but also to benefiting from its hide, bones, and the rest of the carcass.[10]

Izzi Dien's way of problematizing the legal question seems to miss the point, since in the vast majority of cases today species are endangered not because people eat them – indeed, it is the "meat" animals that are in the least danger of becoming extinct – rather, they are endangered because human activities have destroyed their habitats. This is a point that Izzi Dien, one of the Muslim world's leading environmentalist thinkers, inexplicably does not address.

Though al-Sulami's insistence on the primacy of human interests is consistent with the principles of Islamic law, there does exist a basis in the legal tradition for preserving habitats, even if the interests of wildlife *per se* are not the overriding factor. The Qur'an repeatedly emphasizes the importance of "balance" (*mīzān*),[11] and threatens punishment to those who disturb it: "Work no confusion on the earth after it has been set in order."[12] The Qur'anic context would seem to refer mainly to the practices of inter-tribal warfare – destroying the enemy's crops, trees, and livestock – but the principle can be applied by analogy to what is known about ecological balance and biodiversity today.

HUNTING TO EXTINCTION

Despite its prohibition in Islamic law, sport hunting remained a major form of entertainment in Muslim societies, especially among the elites. In Arabia the oryx was hunted to near extinction, and only recently have measures been taken to preserve the species. In Iran, species such as the lion, tiger, and cheetah were hunted into oblivion before modern times, and leopards have become exceedingly rare. Even gazelles, which were the favored game at royal hunting preserves right up until recently, are now generally found only on government lands where private individuals may not enter without special permission.[13]

Historically the most egregious violations of the proscription against sport hunting were in India, where hundreds or thousands of creatures at a time would be indiscriminately slaughtered in bloody orgies of killing for the amusement of the rich and powerful. The favored method (a Central Asian technique called the *qamargha*) was to go out into the wilderness and create a wide circle of "beaters" who would make as much noise as possible as they slowly closed the circle, forcing huge numbers of terrified creatures toward the center. When the circle was almost closed, the royal hunters would fire at will into the throng of panic-stricken animals. So horrific was the resulting bloodbath that at one point the Mughal emperor Akbar the Great (r. 1555–1605) decided enough was enough and banned the sport, though apparently only for a time.

Akbar, however, was not a typical Muslim – in fact he eventually started his own religion – and his awakening to the horrors of mass slaughter seems to have been instigated by some vegetarian Jain advisors.[14] The *Ā'īn-i Akbarī*, a royal gazetteer compiled under Akbar's reign, contains a detailed account of the royal elephants, horses, camels, and other domestic animals, as well as regulations for animal fights (ostensibly forbidden under Islamic law). It has a lengthy section on sport hunting as well (also technically forbidden), even including a section on "hunt-ing deer with deer." Many of the regulations stipulated, such as the branding of horses on the face, are explicit contradictions of Islamic law.[15]

Akbar's chief advisor and chronicler, Abu'l-Fazl Allami, justi-fies the emperor's hunting in the following way:

> Superficial, worldly observers see in killing an animal a sort of pleasure, and in their ignorance stride about, as if senseless, on the field of their passions. But deep inquirers see in hunting a means of acquisition of knowledge, and the temple of their worship derives from it a peculiar luster. This is the case with His Majesty.[16]

Akbar's son and successor, Jahangir (r. 1605–1627), had a keen interest in the natural world and makes many observations about India's wildlife in his memoirs, the *Tuzūk-i Jahangīrī*. His Islam, however, was as selective as his father's, and he often went out on hunts. Jahangir had his record-keepers maintain a meticulous tally of animals killed, and boasts in his memoirs that from the time he was twelve until the age of fifty:

> ... 28,532 animals were taken in my presence. Of this total I shot with my own hand 17,167 animals as follows: quadrupeds, 3,203: lions 86; bear, cheetah, fox, otter, hyena, 9; *nilgai*, 889; *maha*, a species of deer as large and bulky as a nilgai, 35; buck and doe antelope, *chikara*, spot-ted deer, mountain goat, et cetera, 1,672; ram and red deer, 215; wolf, 64; wild ox, 36; boar, 90; ibex, 26; mountain ram, 22; argali sheep, 32; wild ass, 6; hare, 23. Birds, 13,964 as follows: pigeon, 10,348; *lagar-jhagar* hawk, 3; eagle, 2; kite, 23; [*jughd*] owl, 39; pelican, 12; mouse-eater, 5; sparrow, 41; dove, 25; [*bum*] owl, 30; duck, goose, heron, et cetera, 150; crow, 3,473. Aquatic animals: *mag-armachch*, which means crocodile, 10.[17]

Interestingly, the most islamically "orthodox" of the Mughal emperors, Awrangzeb Alamgir (r. 1656–1707), was also an avid sport hunter. The Mughals were only the last and greatest of many Muslim dynasties in India, and though sport hunting was also an activity favored by the British during their two-hundred-year *raj*, the most dramatic reduction in India's wildlife prior to the industrial period probably occurred under the Mughals.

WILDLIFE PRESERVES IN ISLAMIC LAW

The Islamic legal tradition contains two institutions which some contemporary scholars have argued could be considered as forms of wildlife preserve. They are the *himā*, a "protected area" or sanctuary, and the *harīm*, which was a "greenbelt" or easement around settled areas intended mainly to ensure a safe water supply. A related institution, the *harām*, refers to areas around the sacred cities of Mecca and Medina (called the *harāmayn*; "the two forbidden areas") where hunting is outlawed.

The *harāmayn* were apparently established in the Prophet Muhammad's time, when, according to the hadiths, he declared Mecca "sacred by virtue of the sanctity conferred on it by God until the day of resurrection. Its thorn trees shall not be cut down, its game shall not be disturbed . . ."[18] He also made a sanctuary of Medina, whose "trees shall not be cut and its game shall not be hunted."[19]

The prohibition on hunting while on pilgrimage comes from the Qur'an:

Do not kill game when you are in pilgrim sanctity; whoever of you kill it intentionally, there shall be compensation equal to what he has killed from [his] flocks, as two persons of just character among you shall decide – an offering to be delivered at the *kaʿba*.[20]

It would seem from this verse that killing wild animals when one is supposed to be in a state of purity is wrong because it is a crime *against* God, not against the animals in question. One must atone for this by paying the equivalent in one's own domestic livestock "back to God." This atonement for the killing of wild animals by killing yet more domestic animals can hardly be seen to benefit the animals themselves.

But we are asking very different sorts of questions from those pondered by the jurists of the formative period of Islamic law. For al-Shafiʿi, for example, the verse primarily raises the question of what is meant by "equal compensation":

> Equal compensation in kind literally means the nearest in size to the body [of the game killed]. The viewpoints of the Companions of the Apostle who expressed an opinion on game are at one that compensation should be nearest in size to the body of the game. We should therefore examine the game killed, and whatever of the livestock is found to resemble it in size should be paid in compensation.[21]

Clearly the importance here is to show proper respect for God's possessions, not the preservation of wildlife *per se*. Where today a conservation-minded Muslim might ask, "How can we ensure that pilgrims don't hunt the Arabian oryx to extinction?" in the ninth century the concern was over ensuring just compensation "to God" – obviously, two very different contexts and historical conditions. One is led to wonder, however, what it would take to "compensate God" for the unparalleled destruction of habitats and species wrought by humans today!

Some traditional *himā*s still exist in Saudi Arabia, but they are much diminished from former times and continue to disappear. Most of these preserves are aimed at excluding sheep and goats from grazing lands in preference to cattle, camels and donkeys, but others exist to control the cutting of firewood or to keep flowering meadows intact for honeybees.[22]

Even in the *harām*s around the holy cities, species such as the ibex and gazelle are no longer found. In fact the laws pertaining to these preserves have been generally ignored, on the basis that "development" – geared largely to servicing (and fleecing) the millions of pilgrims who now descend on the holy sites – is a need which overrides that of preserving nature.

What is important to note is that these areas were restricted primarily so that they might benefit humans. The *himā*, which in pre-Islamic times was an institution that allowed powerful landowners to keep others off their grazing lands, was transformed in the Prophet Muhammad's time into a means for preserving certain tracts of land for the public benefit. Significantly, the preserved areas were not to be too large, so as not to take too much land "out of circulation."

In short, the institutions of *himā, harīm* and *harām* are all clearly meant to preserve resources for human needs, not those of animals. If animals are preserved, or if they benefit from the preservation of water and vegetation, this is a secondary benefit, as they themselves are seen in the law as existing for the good of humans.

Thus, in order for the institution of *himā* to be revived in Muslim regions today in a form that would actually serve to protect wildlife for the sake of biodiversity and ecosystem balance, the traditional rationale for its existence would have to be reinterpreted in light of contemporary scientific understanding. To date such an effort has not been undertaken, as few if any Islamic legal scholars seem to have ventured into the works of biodiversity specialists such as E. O. Wilson, Niles Eldredge, or Richard Leakey.

The Need for a New Jurisprudence

Most Muslims follow legal rulings laid down during the eighth to tenth centuries, when scholars were busy applying the techniques of jurisprudence (*ijtihād* – literally, "mental struggle") to address problems and issues not explicitly faced by Muhammad and his Companions.

By the end of this period Sunni scholars, feeling that all important legal questions had been resolved, declared the "gates of *ijtihād*" to be closed, and since then Sunni law has tended to imitate the precedents laid down by the classical jurists.[23] This pattern of imitation, known as *taqlīd*, has led to considerable problems in the modern age, with so many new phenomena and issues appearing that are not addressed in the classical legal texts. For example, should women be allowed to drive cars? Should mosques have loudspeakers? Should slavery still be permitted? Can Western democracies serve as a model for "Islamic" governments?

Many contemporary Muslim intellectuals believe that the imitative nature of Sunni law over the past millennium has led to cultural stagnation, and that *ijtihād* must be revived to meet the needs of today's Muslims. The call for renewing the practice of Islamic jurisprudence could be seen as directly relevant to addressing such animal-related issues as factory-farming, genetic modification of organisms, and species preservation, since these are areas where traditional legal models have proven inadequate or obsolete.

Unfortunately this does not yet appear to be the case. Islamic jurists tend to investigate only the questions posed to them by their clients, and thus far, few contemporary Muslims have been moved to ask their jurist of preference to offer opinions on any of the deeper or more troubled aspects of human–animal interaction which have been brought to light by animal rights philosophers and activists. Their questions are mostly limited to whether or not particular meat is lawful for them to eat – a purely self-interested concern.

When today's Islamic jurists are asked to apply *ijtihād* to issues of animal rights, they typically do little more than rehearse the positions of their ancient predecessors. This is as true of Shi'i jurists – for whom the practice of *ijtihād* theoretically never abated – as it is for their Sunni counterparts. Thus, the recent "animal rights" treatises of such scholars as the Iranian Hashem Najy Jazayery, the Kuwaiti Mustafa Mahmud Helmy, and the Indian Ashraf Ali Thanvi are really nothing more than compilations of Qur'an and hadith citations such as those cited in chapter one, accompanied by brief and somewhat obvious commentaries.[24] An older compilation, published by the head jurist of Al-Azhar seminary a century ago under the title *Treatment of Animals in Islamic Law (Al-Rifq bi'l-hayawān fī'l-sharī'a al-islāmiya)*, is currently being distributed by the Society for the Protection of Animal Rights in Egypt (SPARE), and an English version is being prepared by University of Washington law professor Kristen Stilt.[25] While such resources are no doubt valuable, today's conditions would seem to call for more than just reminders of forgotten pre-modern Islamic norms.

What is largely missing now in the world of Islamic jurisprudence is any kind of deeper discourse that engages contemporary understandings of animal rights, factory farming, and species preservation. The main reason for this lack is that the system of Islamic jurisprudence responds only to inputs; that is, Islamic jurists work on whatever questions individual Muslims put to them. Until Muslims start asking their preferred legal experts for opinions on contemporary animal-related issues, the jurists will not waste time on them. A secondary problem is that since so many of these questions today arise from contexts which are entirely new in history, jurists can refer only to precedents where the contexts were dramatically different and may shed little light on those of the present. Finally, the tendency toward resisting new restrictions, on the principle that "all is allowed unless explicitly forbidden," adds a heavy weight of inertia where new understandings of animal rights are concerned.

Islamic law developed during the eighth to tenth centuries to meet the need for a universally accepted code of norms within an exceptionally diverse and cosmopolitan Muslim society. This need is, if anything, even stronger today. Among Muslims, no guiding principle can hope to find universal validation unless it emanates from Islamic law. The process for articulating such principles, however, is constrained by tradition to reliance on the four accepted sources of jurisprudence: the Qur'an, the *sunna*, analogical reasoning (*qiyās*), and the consensus of scholars (*ijma'*).

Thus, even were contemporary jurists to read the works of Peter Singer, Tom Regan, Bernard Rollin, and Evelyn Pluhar, or pay visits to factory farms or scientific laboratories, technically speaking none of these would be admissible sources for the derivation of Islamic laws. It may be, however, that becoming familiar with these contemporary arguments and experiences would enable Islamic jurists to search the accepted sources of jurisprudence with new eyes.

Still, it will be extremely difficult for any eventual animal rights-conscious Muslim jurists (especially in the more *taqlīd*-oriented Sunni tradition) to overcome the longstanding impulse to refer to thousand-year-old models. The most likely resource for an Islamic jurisprudence regarding animals which takes the unprecedented conditions of today into account is the principle of *maslaha*, or "seeking the common good." This is because while there appears to be nothing in Islamic law that would allow for privileging the vital interests of animals when they conflict with human interests (even non-vital ones), there are many aspects of how animals are mistreated today which also have a negative impact on humans as well.

It is there that the principle of *maslaha* can come into play. Factory farms are less likely to be declared un-Islamic because they are abusive of animals, than because Muslims come to understand the consequences of eating drug-ridden meat or living in proximity to huge quantities of untreated animal waste. Unfortunately, to date the principle of *maslaha* has most often been invoked as a way of *overriding* traditional restraints on human activities, by those arguing that the "needs" of human development trump the need to preserve and protect nature.

To engage in the kind of jurisprudence called for by the conditions of the present day will require a boldness and creativity rarely seen among experts in Islamic law over the past ten centuries. Nevertheless, the acceleration of change and innovation which characterize today's world, as well as the rapid deterioration of the natural systems which make both human and non-human animal life possible, all cry out urgently for the attention of contemporary Islamic scholars. It may be hoped that one day soon these experts will get beyond the handing out of pat answers based on thousand-year-old precedents and conditions, and apply their interpretive skills to the unprecedented situations in which humans and the animals affected by their activities find themselves today.

INITIATIVES AT AL-AZHAR

Cairo's venerable Al-Azhar seminary, founded over a thousand years ago, is the most prestigious institution of Sunni learning in the world, and as such the *fatwa*s of its jurists carry a special weight of authority. While the opinions of Al-Azhar's jurists are theoretically no more binding than those of any others and carry no formal enforcement capability, they perhaps come closest to constituting a normative voice for Sunni Muslims. For any Sunni Muslim wanting to persuade other Sunnis of a particular position on a given issue, getting the support of Al-Azhar's chief jurist (known as the *Shaykh al-Azhar*) is a powerful tool.

As early as the 1960s Muslim animal rights activist B. A. al-Masri (whose work will be discussed in chapters five and six) reports that Al-Azhar jurists were presented with the question (by him? He doesn't say) of whether stunning livestock prior to slaughter was acceptable under Islamic law. A committee was formed and came back with a unanimous opinion: that the stunning of livestock is lawful as long as it doesn't interfere with the bleeding procedure prescribed by Islamic law.[26] The committee accepted arguments that stunning animals before killing them was more humane than killing them while they are conscious. They apparently did not consider the unreliability of stunning, the assembly-line conditions normally associated with the use of stunners, nor any other aspect of the issue.

More recently, Al-Azhar has hosted an important conference on animal rights – apparently the first recognized Islamic institution in the world to do so. The conference was organized by Swiss veterinarian Petra Maria Sidhom in collaboration with SPARE, and was held at Al-Azhar's Salih Kamel Center for Islamic Economics in early 2004.

The conference participants, who included scholars of Islamic law, history and philosophy, government officials, veterinarians, and animal rescue workers, called for improved treatment of animals in scientific research, food production, and other areas, as well as for further elaboration of concern for animals from an Islamic perspective. The participants also agreed to undertake certain concrete measures, such as getting slaughterhouses to provide slaughtering services free of charge during 'Id al-Adha (so as to reduce slaughter in the streets), adding "humane slaughter" lectures to the curriculum at Egypt's colleges of agriculture and veterinary medicine, and establishing training sessions for butchers to bring their practices in line with Islamic directives. They urged Egypt's General Organization for Veterinary Sciences (the government agency charged with ensuring the welfare and "development" of animal "resources") to prepare a "Declaration of the Right[s] of Animals" which would take an Islamic point of view, and to make available translations for worldwide distribution. Part of the aim of this would be "to answer unfair accusations directed at Islam and Muslims."[27]

The fact that such discussions are now taking place at an Islamic institution as prestigious and internationally visible as Al-Azhar is highly promising for the future of animal rights initiatives throughout the Muslim world. This is such a recent development, however, that it is impossible to say how far-reaching the results will be.

3

ANIMALS IN PHILOSOPHY AND SCIENCE

Non-human animals are ubiquitous throughout the intellectual and artistic traditions of Muslim civilizations. Almost invariably, however, animal figures were employed as symbols for particular human traits, or were entirely anthropomorphized actors in human-type dramas. In other words, even where non-human animals appear, the real message is about humans. This holds true in the realms of philosophy and mysticism as well as in popular literature and the arts. Only in scientific works, such as treatises on zoology, are animals observed, discussed, and described in their own terms, and even then the emphasis is often on their uses or dangers for humans.

Animals in Islamic Philosophy

Islamic philosophy (*falsafa*) in the early centuries derives primarily from the Hellenistic tradition, known to Muslim intellectuals through translations of famous works from Greek and Aramaic into Arabic. Aristotle's *Historia animalium* was translated into Arabic in the eighth or ninth century, and served, along with much of Aristotle's other work, as a starting point for Muslims engaged in philosophical inquiry.

Abu Nasr Al-Farabi (d. 950), in his *Enumeration of the Sciences (Ihsā' al-'ulūm*, known in medieval Europe through the Latin version of Gerard of Cremona, *De Scientiis*), lists the Science of Animals in the fourth section of his work, under Physics. Like the Greeks, Muslim scholars did not make the disciplinary boundary between philosophy and science that Western academia perceives today; thus, the most well-known intellectual figures often excelled in more than one discipline.

By and large Muslim philosophers were more interested in metaphysical questions (such as the nature and existence of God) than they were in mundane issues like the treatment of animals, the phenomenal world's importance being mainly its potential to illuminate the workings of the Divine Mind. One might even suggest, as their Muslim critics often did, that the philosophers were primarily interested in their *own* minds and intellectual achievements. All in all the philosophical tradition is not a particularly rich place to look for Muslim attitudes about animals, but there are some exceptions.

One example is the Iranian skeptic Rhazes (Abu Bakr Muhammad b. Zakariyya al-Razi, d. 925 or 932), a believer in the transmigration of souls, who addresses the problem of animal slaughter in his book *The Philosophical Way (Sīrat al-falsafīya)*. Rhazes accepts the need for killing wild animals when they pose a risk to human life, but finds it difficult to justify the slaughter of domestic creatures. In the end, however, he rationalizes both cases by claiming that by killing an animal one is liberating its soul and thus allowing it to transmigrate into a superior body, bringing it closer to salvation.[1] It must be noted that Rhazes' views are patently heretical from the perspective of mainstream Islam – indeed, he was accused by his detractors of not being a Muslim at all.

The great philosopher-physician Avicenna (Abu Ali ibn Sina, 980–1037), one of the principal "islamicizers" of the Greek peripatetic tradition, wrote a very short mystical treatise called *The Bird (Al-Tayr)* in which he employs the oft-used symbol of a bird in flight to represent the soul's journey "upward" to find ultimate reality. Avicenna's bird, who narrates his own tale in the first person, is first freed from his cage by other birds; they then all fly away together in search of "the King." Not one of Avicenna's best-known works, *The Bird* may nevertheless have served as inspiration for the celebrated Sufi poetic tale of Farid al-Din Attar, *The Conference of the Birds*, discussed in the following chapter. Both Muhammad Ghazali and his younger brother Ahmad wrote mystical treatises modeled on Avicenna's *The Bird*, as did the illuminationist philosopher Shihab al-din Suhrawardi.[2]

Following Aristotle, Muslim philosophers saw the universe in terms of a "great chain of being," with inanimate matter at the bottom and progressing upwards through plants, animals, and humans, to angels, and finally to God Himself. Each stage is seen as being more developed and more perfect than the last. This hierarchy, based as it is on an originally pagan worldview, corresponds to that found in the Qur'an and, for that matter, in Western Christian culture as well.

Muslim philosophers and Sufis also follow the Greeks in distinguishing between the "animal soul" and the "rational soul," the latter being uniquely found in humans. The former is located in the heart and, being material, is subject to eventual destruction. The latter, by contrast, is immaterial and eternal. In the mind of many Muslim philosophers and mystics, it is the aim of the rational soul to be re-united with Universal Reason (that is to say, God). Non-human animals, lacking this "rational soul," cannot aspire to eternal life in union with the Divine.

THE CASE OF THE ANIMALS VERSUS MAN

The so-called "Pure Brethren" (*Ikhwān al-safā'*) were a group of radical Muslim philosophers who lived and wrote in the southern Iraqi city of Basra during the latter third of the tenth century. Their very name contains an animal reference, as it is borrowed from a fable about a group of doves in the *Kalila and Dimna* stories (which will be discussed in chapter four). The Brethren wrote their treatises collectively and – due probably to the unorthodox nature of many of their positions – anonymously.

The best-known of their fifty-one works, *The Case of the Animals versus Man before the King of the Jinn*, is probably the most extensive critique of mainstream human attitudes towards animals in the entire vast corpus of Muslim literature.

In this unusual book, representatives from the animal kingdom bring a court case against the human race whom they accuse of abusing their superior position. The animals point out that before the creation of man they roamed the earth in peace and harmony – what might be called in contemporary language "natural balance" – until the arrival of humans who do nothing but exploit and destroy and who lack any sense of justice:

> We were fully occupied in caring for our broods and rearing our young with all the good food and water God had allotted us, secure and unmolested in our own lands. Night and day we praised and sanctified God, and God alone.
>
> Ages passed and God created Adam, father of mankind, and made him his vice-regent on earth. His offspring reproduced, and his seed multiplied. They spread over the earth – land and sea, mountain and plain. Men encroached on our ancestral lands. They captured sheep, cows, horses, mules, and asses from among us and enslaved them, subjecting them to the exhausting toil and drudgery of hauling, being ridden, plowing, drawing water, and turning mills. They forced us to these things under duress, with beatings, bludgeonings, and every kind of torture and chastisement our whole lives long. Some of us fled to deserts, wastelands, or mountaintops, but the Adamites pressed after us, hunting us with every kind of wile and device. Whoever fell into their hands was yoked, haltered, and fettered. They slaughtered and flayed him, ripped open his belly, cut off his limbs and broke his bones, tore out his eyes; plucked his feathers or sheared off his hair or fleece, and put him onto the fire to be cooked, or on the spit to be roasted, or subjected him to even more dire tortures, whose full extent is beyond description. Despite these cruelties, these sons of Adam are not through with us but

must claim that this is their inviolable right, that they are our masters and we are their slaves, deeming any of us who escapes a fugitive, rebel, shirker of duty – all with no proof or explanation beyond sheer force.[3]

The trial proceeds as the humans present one argument after another to support their claims of uniqueness and entitlement. Though the humans insist that "philosophical and rational proofs" will be used to establish their case, the evidence they bring fails to live up to this promise. "Our beautiful form, the erect construction of our bodies, our upright carriage, our keen senses, the subtlety of our discrimination, our keen minds and superior intellects all prove that we are masters and they slaves to us," they say.[4] Each of these subjective assessments is demolished in turn through counter-examples provided by the animal plaintiffs, but the humans persist in providing more of the same. "We buy and sell them, give them their feed and water, clothe and shelter them from heat and cold . . ."[5] This justification too, the animals eloquently refute.

The humans then turn to character assassination, criticizing the qualities of various species such as the rabbit, the pig, the horse. Each of these maligned species speaks up in its own defense, richly describing the special qualities and merits of its kind. In every case the animals are the ones providing the rational arguments, in contrast to the humans' arrogant, self-serving and unjustified claims.

Fearing they may be losing the case, the humans begin to contemplate bribing the judges and other sneaky behavior. The animals, meanwhile, hold councils according to their kind – predators, birds, sea creatures, crawling things – and consult with one another respectfully and democratically to elect a representative from each animal category to present their case to the King of the Jinn.

In the discussion among things that crawl, the Brethren go so far as to challenge the example of the Prophet in their defense of animals' right to live. Where Muhammad included poisonous snakes among creatures that Muslims should kill, the Brethren's snake spokesman points out that snakes too play a vital role in the natural community, both as predators keeping other species in check and in producing poisons that not only kill but have medicinal uses as well.

The Brethren recognize that in the world of creation every species plays its assigned role and knows its proper place, with the sole exception of humans. In fact the Brethren's understanding of natural processes and relationships is sophisticated enough that they are sometimes claimed to have foreshadowed Darwin.[6] Yet while one can see in their cosmology an ecological vision that is in some respects strikingly modern, they were creationists, not evolutionists; animals occupy specific vital niches not because they have evolved into them through natural selection, but because God in the perfection of His creative plan has distributed them that way.[7]

On another level it could be argued that *The Case of the Animals versus Man* is an almost post-modern work, in that non-human animals are presented as subjects of their own experience, not merely as objects observed by humans. At least that is the apparent reading up until the last page of the book. But the persuasiveness through which the reader is made sympathetic to the animals' view only makes the culminating scene more shocking: the King of the Jinn, in the end, decides in favor of the humans, basing his judgment on nothing more than the capricious, unproven, and contested premise that humans alone can have eternal life.

This unexpected, abrupt and, from an animal rights perspective, highly unsatisfying conclusion leaves one wondering just what point the Brethren were trying to make. Is their treatise intended to awaken the reader to a non-anthropocentric reality? If so, the ending is clearly unacceptable. But if the intention is to re-assert the view of human uniqueness, why so convincingly make the case on the animals' behalf? Or is the reader's frustration meant to be turned against God, for having established the hierarchy of creation on the basis of such unfair and arbitrary principles? The question is not easily resolved.

Whatever the ultimate intentions of the authors, *The Case of the Animals versus Man* remains quite distinctive in the context of Muslim society, as much today as during the century in which it was written.[8] It is important to note that the views of the Pure Brethren were never accepted into the mainstream of Islamic thought, and that in subsequent centuries, only the heterodox Isma'ili Shi'i sect,[9] identified today with the Aga Khan, adopted their writings as authoritative. Yet it may be that in regard to animal rights, the Pure Brethren (like St. Francis in Catholicism) were simply ahead of their time, and as such they may have more to teach us in the twenty-first century than they did to Muslims of their own era.

ALIVE, SON OF AWAKE

Another philosophical treatise notable for the presence of animal figures is the twelfth-century allegorical novel *Alive, Son of Awake* (*Hayy ibn Yaqzān*), by the philosopher and polymath Muhammad ibn 'Abd al-Malik ibn Tufayl (d. 1185). The story is about a human baby, named Alive, who grows up alone on a desert island in the East Indies. (He is said to have been either spontaneously generated there, or else packed off by his mother in a raft like the baby Moses.)[10] The infant is rescued by a deer who has lost her fawn. Alive grows up among the animals of the island and lives as one of them:

> They say that this roe lived in good and abundant pasture so that she was fat, and had such plenty of milk, that she was very well able to maintain the little child. She stayed by him and never left him, but when hunger forced her. And he grew so acquainted with her, that if at any time she stayed away from him a little longer than ordinary, he'd cry pitifully, and she, as soon as she heard him, came running instantly. Besides all this, he enjoyed this happiness, and there was no beast of prey in the whole island.[11]

As the boy matures, however, he begins to sense that he is somehow "different":

> He considered all the several sorts of animals, and saw that they were all clothed either with hair, wool, or feathers. He considered their great swiftness and strength, and that they

were all armed with weapons defensive, as horns, teeth, hoofs, spurs, and nails, but that he himself was naked and defenseless, slow and weak, in respect of them. For whenever there happened any controversy about gathering of fruits, he always came off by the worst, for they could both keep their own, and take away his, and he could neither beat them off nor run away from them.[12]

The death of Alive's adoptive deer mother stimulates his "natural" scientific curiosity, and the desire to perform an autopsy so as better to understand the phenomenon of death leads him to "invent" rudimentary surgical tools. Eventually, entirely on his own, Alive discovers fire and how to use it, how to domesticate horses, and how to make and use all manner of implements to ensure his survival.

Ibn Tufayl's "ontogeny follows phylogeny" allegory is meant to serve as a backdrop for extrapolating his own neo-Platonic philosophy, but his use of animals is typical. Though animals are portrayed as living harmoniously and serve as an example of the perfection of God's creation, their real importance is to exist as a category from which the human, Alive, can be differentiated. Alive's life journey distinguishes him from the beasts among whom he matures, allowing him "naturally" to "rise above" them and assume his proper place in the cosmic hierarchy, bridging the animal and celestial realms.

Scientific Works on Animals

Muslim scientists composed numerous important treatises on zoology. Among the first of these were specialized studies on camels, sheep, horses, and other species by the Arab writer Abu Sa'id 'Abd al-Malik al-Asma'i (d. 828). His contemporary, Abu 'Ubaida, claimed to have written a fifty-volume work on horses, but this has not survived. A. S. G. Jayakar notes that these were not works based on original scientific research, but merely compilations of existing knowledge.[13] In the following decades several works on natural history appeared in Arabic, falsely attributed to Aristotle. (The high regard in which many Muslim scholars held the Greek philosopher led to many works being spuriously attributed to him.)

The best-known Muslim work on zoology is the seven-volume *Book of Animals* (*Kitāb al-hayawān*) by the ninth-century writer al-Jahiz. Other classical Arabic works on animals include Abu Yahya al-Qazwini's *Wonders of Creation*, al-Marwazi's *Natures of Animals*, ibn Bakhtishu's *Benefits of Animals*, Hamdallah al-Mustawfi al-Qazwini's *Delights of the Heart*, and ibn Duraihim's *Lives of Animals*. The fourteenth-century opus of Kamal al-din al-Damiri, also titled *Lives of Animals*, is largely a commentary on and expansion of al-Jahiz. In all of these works the emphasis is on how various animal species can serve humans, whether for medical purposes or for drawing moral lessons from their example, or for better understanding the mind of the God who created them.

THE *BOOK OF ANIMALS*

The highly prolific Iraqi man of letters Abu 'Uthman 'Amr ibn Bahr al-Fuqaymi al-Basri al-Jahiz (776–869) is one of the most famous figures in Arabic literature. His incomplete seven-volume *Book of Animals* is only one of some two hundred of his written works, but it is perhaps the best known. Typical of Muslim literature, al-Jahiz's use of animals is instrumental: although ostensibly a comprehensive zoological catalogue, the *Book of Animals* aims primarily at demonstrating the magnificence of God through a study of his created beings.

In some respects al-Jahiz's ideas were well ahead of their time, anticipating such things as the theory of evolution and the influence of climate on animal psychology.[14] The fact that he describes the kangaroo (or at least some large marsupial) indicates that even in the ninth century, Middle Eastern Muslims possessed information on the fauna of far-off Australia, thanks to their Indian Ocean trade networks.[15]

In other areas, however, al-Jahiz was little more than a transmitter of folklore. He reports, for example, that the giraffe originated as a hybrid between the camel and the hyena.[16] He relies heavily on information gathered from Bedouin nomads, whom he sees as reliable sources since they spend their lives surrounded by wild animals, even though "their memory is sometimes faulty" and their knowledge of animals is "nothing more to them than a source of income."[17] He believes in the theory of spontaneous generation (of such things as flies, worms, fish, frogs and scorpions), and considers those who disagree to be ignoramuses.[18]

In his scholarly approach al-Jahiz draws heavily on Aristotle's *History of Animals*, although he frequently and mockingly "corrects" the Greek philosopher's information. He writes, for example,

> I was extremely surprised when reading Aristotle's description of the elephant. He notes the large size of the head and the neck which is too short, but he fails to emphasize the fact that the tongue points inward, whereas this is surely the most astonishing trait of all. Neither does he give the period of gestation in the female, nor the weight the tusks can reach, nor the fact that they are born already having their teeth.[19]

The Arab writer seems to have been working with an incomplete text of Aristotle's book, since in fact the Greek philosopher does mention several of these things.

Al-Jahiz derives his taxonomy largely from that of the Qur'an. He divides animals into three broad categories: "Walking animals," including humans, non-carnivorous quadrupeds (*bahā'im*), and carnivorous quadrupeds (*sibā'*); "Flying things" (*tayr*), including noble, ordinary, "less armed," and "small" carnivorous birds, non-carnivorous birds, and flying insects; and finally, "Crawling things" (*hasharāt*) – that is, non-flying insects, snakes, and the like.[20]

In other words, al-Jahiz's classification scheme derives from their habits of eating and locomotion, which allows for a mixing of mammals, birds, reptiles, amphibians, and invertebrates within the same category. He gives little attention to fish, claiming that too little is known about them. Al-Jahiz complains that most information on aquatic animals comes from sailors, who "are people who do not reflect on the implications of what they are talking about and who do not consider the ethics of their acts." His belief – which some would say is not without basis – is that sailors and fishermen are prone to exaggerate their fantastic tales of sea creatures.[21]

The importance given to whether a creature is carnivorous or not suggests an anthropocentric sense of priorities: one of the most important things to know about a given species is whether or not it poses any danger to humans. More important still, from al-Jahiz's point of view, is the fact that all animals – indeed all of Creation – are miraculous signs of God which offer valuable lessons for our own salvation. For, as he writes

> ... the animal that one thinks the least useful of all may turn out to be, perhaps, the most useful, if not in terms of the life below then to that of the life to come ... Therefore, if you notice that an animal is uninterested in providing any service to humans, inapt and unwilling to render any aid or assistance, or even very much a pest ... know that their usefulness resides in the fact that they constitute a test, a difficulty, which God Almighty – may He be exalted and glorified – has prepared precisely to test the endurance and patience of humans ... The reflective man will perceive the purpose to which is served the creation of the scorpion, and what value the Divine Work has placed in that of the snake. May he not despise, therefore, the mosquito, the butterfly, nor ants and flies. Pause to reflect ... you will surely be filled with praise for the Almighty for having created flying insects, crawling things, and animals with fangs and venom; just as you will praise Him for having created the nourishments of the earth, the waters, and the air.[22]

Al-Jahiz takes ample note of the fact that various animal species are better-equipped for a wide range of tasks than humans are:

> The Most-High has given them an extraordinary ease, in their knowledge and abilities, endowing them with beaks and paws, opening up to them a whole range of familiarities in proportion to the tools He has given them, creating

in many species very highly developed sensory organs which render them capable of carrying out prodigious works of art. Without having previously received any preparation, training, education, or apprenticeship, lacking any repeated or graduated practice, these animal species are able, spontaneously, to improvise and execute acts so rapidly and suddenly, that the best informed thinkers and the most erudite philosophers, even if they possess able hands or have access to tools, are incapable of accomplishing them.[23]

Nevertheless, following the standard Qur'anic interpretation of his time, al-Jahiz accepts without question the received cosmic hierarchy which places humans above all other animals, due to what he calls their capacity for reason and their "mastery" (*tamkīn*).

As an example of the kind of "moral lessons" that animals can offer to humans, al-Jahiz offers the story of the Qadi and the Fly, a tale about a highly respected judge who tries to retain his composure while being harassed by a fly as the courtroom looks on. Eventually he begins to swat in vain at the fly, which repeatedly dodges the judge's hand and just as quickly returns to settle on his nose. Finally the judge blurts out, "God forgive me! . . . I have just understood that whereas I enjoyed such respect and dignity among people, I have been defeated and ridiculed by the lowest of His creatures!"[24]

Under the heading of "swine" al-Jahiz attempts to deal rationally with the fact that the Scriptures speak of God transforming humans into pigs and monkeys. One question that arises is why the Qur'an prohibits the consumption of pork, but not of monkeys. Al-Jahiz believes that this is because the formerly Christian Arab tribes were enthusiastic pork eaters, while monkeys were naturally unappealing enough not to require a prohibition. (He offers the same opinion in regard to dogs.)[25] Al-Jahiz opines that those who love pork are unaware of the fact that pigs consume feces.[26]

Though the information in *Kitāb al-hayawān* is of mixed reliability, and despite the fact that al-Jahiz's voluminous work actually contains many digressions that have nothing to do with animals at all, it served as a reference point for virtually all subsequent Muslim writers on animal-related issues and remains widely known and cited today.

THE LIVES OF ANIMALS

Muhammad ibn Musa ibn 'Isa Kamal al-din al-Damiri was Cairene scholar of the Shafi'i school who lived from 1341 to 1405. His *Lives of Animals* (*Hayāt al-hayawān al-kubra*) is his most famous work. He states that his motivation in writing the book – an encyclopedic treatment containing 1,069 entries – was "to correct false notions about animals" that existed in his time,[27] though he perpetuated quite a few of them himself (such as the belief that the rhinoceros was a cross-breed between a horse and an elephant). As with al-Jahiz, the entries are organized alphabetically by animal names, and provide commentary on the origin of each name, physical and behavioral descriptions of each animal, references in the hadiths, whether it is lawful for Muslims to eat, proverbs connected with it, its medicinal properties, and its significance in dreams.

Al-Damiri makes frequent reference to al-Jahiz's work, which seems to have been his major source. Al-Damiri's entries, however, include more detailed descriptions of the individual species than those of al-Jahiz, whose interests were more philological. Like his predecessor, al-Damiri incorporated much spurious material, including references to mythical animals such as the Buraq, the horse-like creature which, according to Muslim folklore, served as the Prophet Muhammad's mount during his miraculous night journey (*mi'rāj*) to heaven.

The following excerpt from al-Damiri's first entry, on the lion (*asad*), gives a sense for the nature of his zoological encyclopedia:

> Lion. One of the well-known beasts of prey. It is mentioned in a tradition (*sunna*, that is, a hadith) of Umm Zar',
> "My husband, if he goes inside is a lynx and if he comes
> forth is a lion." It has several names. Ibn Khalawayh says
> that the lion has five hundred names descriptive of it, and

'Ali ibn Qasim ibn Ja'far the lexicographer has added one hundred and thirty more to them . . . The fact of possessing several names indicates the nobility of the one that is named . . .

Its canine teeth are prominent and projecting, because it is the noblest of all wild animals, for its position among them is that of a dreaded king, on account of its strength, its boldness, the hardness of its heart, its agility, the austere appearance of its countenance, and the malignity of its nature. For this reason also, it is employed in proverbs to express strength, boldness, valor, impetuosity in attacking, bravery, and ferocity. On that account Hamza ibn 'Abd al-Muttalib was called "the lion of God" (*Asadullah*); but it is also said that this name for Hamza ibn 'Abd al-Muttalib as well as Abu Qatada the horseman of the Prophet, is derived from the nobleness of the lion. It is mentioned in the *Sahīh* of Muslim, in the chapter on the subject of giving a killer or murderer the plundered property of the person killed, that [the first Caliph] Abu Bakr said, "Never, by God, we shall not give it to the hyenas of the Quraysh [the pagan Meccan tribe to which Muhammad had belonged], but we shall call a lion of the lions of God, to fight in His and His Apostle's cause" . . .

The lion is of several kinds. Aristotle says, "I have seen a kind in which the face is like that of a man, the body is intensely red, and the tail resembles that of a scorpion" . . . Another kind has the appearance of a cow, with black horns nearly a span in length. The authors of books treating on the subject of natures of animals say as regards the well-known beast of prey – the lion – that its female gives birth to only one whelp at a time which at its birth is only a mass of flesh without any sense of feeling or movement; she watches it in this state for three days, at the end of which period the male parent comes to it and blows into its mouth several times till it begins to breathe and move; its limbs then become loose and it takes the appearance of the male parent. The dame then comes and suckles it but it does not open its eyes until after seven days from its birth. When it is six months old it has to learn to obtain its own prey. They say that the lion is very patient of hunger, and does not stand much in need of water, which two qualities are not found in any of the other beasts of prey. As a sign of the nobleness of its character it may be mentioned that it never eats a prey killed by another and that when it has satisfied its hunger with its own prey, it leaves and does not return to it. When it is hungry it becomes vexed, but when its stomach is full it is pleased. It never drinks water or of that which a dog has lapped. A poet alludes to this particularity with these words:

> I forsake her love, not from hatred for her
> But because there are many sharers in it
> When flies sit on food
> I take my hand away from it, even when I have craving
> for it
> And lions eschew places of water
> Wherein dogs have thrust their muzzles.

. . . When it eats, it simply tears its food with the fore-teeth but does not chew it, and it has very little saliva. On this account it is said to have a stinking breath.[28] It is described as brave and cowardly at the same time; as instances of its cowardice, it may be mentioned that it is afraid of the crowing of a cock, of the noise of a basin, of the yowl of a cat, and that it becomes confused at the sight of a fire. It is very powerful and violent, and does not associate with any other beasts of prey, because it considers none of them equal to it; when its skin falls on any of them, the hair of the beast on which it falls drops off. It never approaches a menstruating woman even if driven to an extremity. It is always in a heated or a feverish state and lives to a long age, the sign of its old age being the falling off of its teeth.

Ibn Sabʿ al-Sabti relates in *Shifaʾ al-sudūr* regarding ʿAbdullah ibn ʿUmar ibn al-Khattab, that while he was on one of his travels, he saw a body of people standing on the way, whereupon he asked as to what the matter was, and being told that a lion on the road had frightened them, he dismounted and going to it, seized it by its ear and moved it out of the way; he then spoke to it and said, "Verily, the Prophet has not lied in his words, that thou hast obtained an ascendancy over man, because of his fear for any being but God, but if man were to fear God, thou wouldst not overpower him, and if man had feared none but God, the Blessed and High, he would not have deputed that power to another." It is mentioned in the *Sunān* of Abu Dawud, out of a tradition of 'Abd al-Rahman ibn Adam, without any other authority with him on the matter, on the authority of Abu Hurayra, that the Prophet said, " 'Isa ibn Maryam [Jesus son of Mary] will descend to the earth, water trickling down his head without wetting him; he will break the cross, kill the pig, and cause wealth to abound, when safety and security will prevail on the earth, so much so that the lion and the camel, the tiger and the cow, the wolves and goats will graze together, and boys will play with snakes, but not one of them will hurt another. 'Isa will remain on the earth for forty years and then die, when the Muslims will say a prayer over him and bury him" . . .[29]

Al-Damiri goes on to relate further hadiths which contain references to lions, then digresses into several pages about remedies for fear (the connection presumably being that this is an affliction from which lions do not generally suffer). He finally returns to the topic of lions under the subheading "Their Lawfulness [to eat]," in which he takes note of the numerous hadiths stating that the flesh of carnivores (defined as animals with fangs) is not lawful.

In the next section of the entry al-Damiri lists popular expressions associated with lions, which include, "More honored than the lion," "Bigger than a lion," "Braver than a lion," and "More stinking in breath than a lion." He then discusses the beneficial properties of things taken from the lion, such as smearing one's whole body with lion fat so as to ward off dangerous predators.

Al-Damiri claims that if an epileptic child wears a lionskin he will be cured, but that after puberty this remedy is ineffective. A person carrying a lion's tail will be immune from the plotting of evildoers. Lion bile applied to the eyelids is said to sharpen one's sight, and powdered lion's testicles mixed with borax and drunk in a barley solution will cure all manner of stomach ailments. Dried lion excrement, mixed in oil, is recommended as a cure for vitiligo, and if drunk can cure alcoholism.[30]

The final aspect of al-Damiri's discussion on lions has to do with their appearance in dreams. Generally (and not surprisingly) dream-lions are a symbol of authority and strong rule, though a dream about wrestling with a lion "may sometimes indicate illness," and dreaming of holding a lion cub foretells that one's wife will bear a son. If one dreams of eating the head of a lion, he may look forward to acquiring a kingdom.[31]

Al-Damiri's encyclopedia remained a standard reference up to modern times.[32] Later additions to Muslim knowledge of zoology came largely from India, especially in the Mughal period. The founder of that dynasty, Zahir al-din Muhammad Babur (1483–1530), a descendent of Tamerlane, was originally from Central Asia, and had a keen eye for the natural wonders of his adopted country. His memoirs, the *Baburnama*, contain a wealth of observation about the fauna and flora of India. Among the indigenous animals he describes are the elephant, the rhinoceros, the nilgai, the crocodile, the peacock, the parrot, and many others.[33]

Babur's grandson, Akbar the Great, and great-grandson Jahangir, both mentioned in chapter two, carried on the tradition of composing detailed memoirs which covered many aspects of life in India, including descriptions of animals. Akbar's royal gazetteer, the *Ā'īn-i Akbarī*, gives descriptions of animals to rival those in the zoological works discussed above. In fact, in the case of animals native to India, the information provided is often far superior,[34] and superseded only by the later work of British and contemporary Indian zoologists.

In conclusion, the philosophical and scientific literature of the Muslim world is rich in information about and references to animals, and added much to our general knowledge as well as to the world of animal imagery. At the same time, Muslim philosophers and scientists, consistent with those of other traditions, perceived and discussed animals primarily through the lens of human interests and concerns.

4

ANIMALS in LITERATURE and ART

Non-human animals appear throughout the literary and artistic production of Muslims, just as in most human cultures. It is important to note, however, that we are entering here into the realm of popular culture. That is to say, though the material in question is produced by Muslims, it may have little or nothing to do with Islam. For example, much of the subject matter is highly salacious, even by modern standards. Many of the scenes in which animals appear are situations where they are witness to human misbehaviors, such as the dog who finds his mistress in bed with his master's friend, or the parrot who tries to prevent his owner's wife from visiting her lover in his absence.

Most such stories are more entertaining than instructive, offering more titillation than morals. (The good do not always win!) Moreover, much of the representational art of Muslim societies is in the form of illustrations accompanying works of popular literature done for courtly elites. In Islamic law, there is a tendency towards iconoclasm, and the kind of figurative images found in book paintings are mostly condemned by

Islamic religious scholars. Nevertheless, popular literature and art are some of the most visible, widely-known, and evocative aspects of the cultures Muslims live in, often more so than texts and norms that are strictly "religious."

Animals in Muslim Literature

As in the philosophical texts described in the previous chapter, animals in the popular literature and art of Muslim societies are most often used as embodiments of specific human traits – lions for bravery, foxes for cunning, donkeys for stupidity, peacocks for vanity – and for purposes of teaching moral lessons relevant to humans. Works which refer to actual animals in their own right and on their own terms are extremely rare.

In fact animal characters are mostly, though not always, mere caricatures of humans. Some writers do display a keen awareness of real animal traits, behaviors, and interests. Still, in most cases it is clear that the presentation of animals in Muslim literature is metaphorical. Animals also figure in common poetic expressions such as "the bird of his soul flew from the nest of his body" (in other words, "he died"), and in proverbs such as "If you take Jesus' donkey to Mecca, when it gets there it will still be a donkey" (Sa'di) and "One cannot expect a donkey to dance or a camel to take a bath" (Nakhshabi).

Animals in Arabic Literature

From pre-Islamic times camels and camel references figure prominently in the poetic tradition of the Arabs. (This is perhaps not a surprising phenomenon, given the importance of this animal in the Bedouin economy.) The Arab poets praised the camel's endurance, speed, and rhythmic gait – indeed, certain poetic meters seem to reflect the lumbering walk of this "ship of the desert."

Not all references to animals in Bedouin poetry were positive, however. The Bedouin were great satirists who loved to ridicule their enemies through verse, as do mutually antagonistic Arab groups today. A favored insult was to accuse someone of eating animal genitals:

> What would you like better, Fazara, a Sayhani date with some clarified butter, or a donkey's prick?
> O yes, Fazara prefers a donkey's prick and its balls to Fazara itself![1]

Among the early Muslim poets to make references to animals, an Abbasid bureaucrat (possibly an Iranian who wrote in Arabic), Qasim Yusuf ibn Qasim (fl. ca. 840), is remarkable for his elegies to birds, cats, and goats. The following verses are typical of him:

> O my eyes weep copiously for our goat, Sawda ["Blackie"]
> Who was like a good-looking bride on the day of marriage.
> She had two smooth thin horns and two teats like filled buckets;
> Her neck and eyes resembled those of the young wild gazelle;
> Her ears were long, face oval, and teeth sparkled when she smiled.
> . . .
> You were a living cloud, a spring-tide, you deserve good praise.
> If the living men could redeem the dead by payment of ransom,
> We would have redeemed you whatever the price.
> O Sawda, you were very good, would that you had lived longer.[2]

These and similar poems would seem to be about actual animals known to the poet, as opposed to the instrumental and symbolic uses of animals in most Muslim literature. Qasim's expressions of deep attachment for specific individual animals are thus rather unusual, although another early poet, Muhammad ibn Yasir, also wrote verses praising pets.[3]

A much better-known Arabic poet, the Syrian Abu'l-'Ala al-Ma'arri (973–1058), composed a work titled *The Treatise of the Horse and the Mule (Risālat al-sāhil wa'l-shāhij)*, in which talking mules, donkeys, horses, camels and foxes have lives and concerns of their own and even consider complaining to the king about their mistreatment. For example, the camel describes the ruthless manner in which his species is treated by the Bedouin:

> One of the strange acts of humans is that, when they want to travel in a country without water, they deprive the camels of water for eight days, then, when they are all but exhausted from thirst, they let them drink their fill. Then they go into the desert; and if water is scarce, they cut their bellies open and drink the liquid contained in it . . . They drink our blood, which they let in times of drought . . . No animal has to suffer from humans what camels have to suffer; they exhaust them while traveling, and feed them in the desert to beasts and birds of prey . . .[4]

The parallels with *The Case of the Animals versus Man* are striking, and like the Pure Brethren, al-Ma'arri seems to have at least dabbled in esoteric Isma'ili ideas.[5]

In another work, *The Treatise of Forgiveness (Risālat al-ghufrān)*, al-Ma'arri expresses the belief that the animals in heaven will not only be those that are there as a backdrop for good humans (that is, to serve as prey for heavenly hunting trips), but also animals who have earned eternal life through their sufferings on earth. This notion, too, would have struck most of al-Ma'arri's contemporaries as shockingly unorthodox.

KALILA AND DIMNA

Perhaps the best-known animal stories in Muslim societies are found in the Iranian translator Ibn al-Muqaffa's ninth-century rendering from Middle Persian to Arabic of *Kalila and Dimna*, a collection of animal fables which came to pre-Islamic Iran from India.[6] The general plot, connecting the various stories which occur as continuous digressions, follows the fortunes of two jackal brothers, Kalila and Dimna, at the court of the lion king. As in George Orwell's political allegory *Animal Farm*, the stories are really about people and politics and contain only the barest and most superficial observations about the traits of actual animals.

Dimna, the more ambitious of the two jackal brothers, decides to take advantage of his natural cunning and offers his services as adviser to the lion king, despite Kalila's warning to stay out of politics. Dimna is accepted at court, and joins the king's inner circle. His first challenge is to advise the king on how to deal with the presence of a menacing-looking newcomer, a large bull grazing in a nearby field. Dimna offers his advice in the form of a fable, telling the king about a fox who comes upon a drum hanging in a tree and, not knowing what it is, rips it open and finds there is nothing inside. Likewise, he suggests, the bull may be nothing more than an empty threat.

With Dimna acting as go-between, the lion and the bull make contact and eventually become great friends. Dimna, dismayed at being displaced from the king's affections, begins to plot against the bull. In discussing his problem with Kalila, the two jackals exchange one tale after another to make their various points.

For example, Dimna illustrates the fact that the weak can conquer the strong through cleverness by telling the tale of a crow whose eggs are repeatedly eaten by a snake. At first the crow considers trying to peck the snake's eyes out while he is asleep, but her friend the jackal warns that this is risky. In his turn, he tells a story of some fish whose pond is about to be drained; they ask a crane to ferry them to safety, but the crane merely carts them off to a place where he can eat them at his leisure. Upon hearing this cautionary tale, the crow decides that instead of attacking the snake herself, she will get some humans to do it by stealing a necklace from them and dropping it down the snake's hole. Sure enough, the humans come out and finish off the snake, and the crow's eggs are safe.

Dimna's attempts to poison the ears of the lion king against his friend the bull also take the form of animal fables. The tale of the three fish and the fishermen, in which only the wise fish wastes no time before escaping, moves the king to an attitude of prudence. Dimna continues with the story of the bedbug and the flea, in which a seemingly insignificant flea makes his more visible friend the bedbug pay the penalty for their joint crime of devouring a sleeping woman's luscious flesh. This tale persuades the king that his own friend, the peaceful, herbivorous bull, cannot be trusted.

Not content with turning the king against his dearest companion, Dimna then proceeds to incite the bull against the king, pointing out that lions are carnivores and eat herbivores like the bull. Recalling the story of the lion and the camel, in which a sickly camel takes refuge with a lion but at the instigation of the lion's fellow carnivores becomes a meal nevertheless, the bull falls into despair. Through a further set of tales, Dimna persuades the bull to launch a surprise attack on the lion king before the lion attacks him.

Of course, in the end the lion kills the bull, though immediately afterwards he is stricken with remorse for doing so. Kalila, disgusted by his brother's treachery, disowns Dimna forever, but that is the extent of the latter's punishment and Dimna regains his position as the lion king's adviser. The outcome is hardly morally satisfying. If there is an overriding theme in the Kalila and Dimna stories, it is that no animal can act contrary to its nature, and that no one can really be trusted – the law of the jungle! Needless to say, this is not an Islamic teaching, but it surely represents the way many medieval Muslims viewed the world they lived in.

THE *THOUSAND AND ONE NIGHTS*

The well-known tales found in the *Thousand and One Nights* (*Alf layla wa layla*; also known, erroneously, as the *Arabian Nights*), contain many animal characters. Like *Kalila and Dimna*, most of the *Thousand and One Nights* stories came into Arabic through Persian, though there is no definitive version and stories were added to the collection right up until recent times.

The basic plot is that an ancient Persian king, Shahryar, has been cuckolded by his wife, a typically faithless woman with an irrepressible hankering for well-endowed black slaves. As merely killing the queen would not be nearly revenge enough for this abominable dishonor, the humiliated king decides to take a new virgin bride every day and have her executed at night. The country seems in danger of losing all its young women to this royal psychopath, until the prime minister's brilliant daughter, Scheherezade (Shahrzad, in its original Persian spelling), volunteers to marry the king. She tells him an enthralling tale through the night, but leaves off at dawn; the king, eager to hear the rest, spares her another day. The cycle continues for a thousand and one nights, until the king realizes he has fallen in love with the ravishing young story-teller and decides not to kill her after all. (Presumably Shahrzad, for her part, has somehow come to see the attractive side of her serial killer husband, but this is never explained.)

Most of the stories center on human heroes, such as Aladdin, Ali Baba, and Sindbad the Sailor. When animal figures do appear, they are not always animals. In the Tale of the Donkey, for example, two thieves steal a man's donkey when he isn't looking and one of them puts the beast's lead around his own neck. He tells the owner he is a man who was transformed into a donkey because of his sins. The foolish owner believes him and sets him free, only to see his actual donkey for sale at the marketplace the following day. Assuming the "man" has sinned again, he reprimands the donkey, "I won't buy you a second time"![7]

In other stories, humans really are turned into animals, as in the tale of the Fisherman and the Genie. In this story, a fisherman catches fish of four colors. Later, as the fish are being cooked in the royal kitchen, an apparition of a beautiful girl appears and asks them if they are "still faithful." "Yes, yes, we are faithful!" they reply. The scene repeats itself several times, to the astonishment of all at court. Eventually it emerges that the fish are the former subjects of an adulterous queen (is there any other kind?), the scapegoat victims of a vengeful curse.[8]

Likewise, the dervish in the Tale of the Porter and the Three Girls of Baghdad is turned into an ape by an angry genie. The hapless dervish takes refuge on a ship and impresses the captain with a demonstration of fine calligraphy. The dervish-ape's talents win him the attention of the king; he writes poems for the monarch and beats him at chess. Eventually, the king's daughter perceives that the ape is really a man. As she happens to be a skilled sorceress, she changes him back into his original form.[9]

Apes appear as well in the Tale of Khalifa the Fisherman. In this case the apes have been transformed not from humans, but from fish. For reasons that are never explained, they send the fisherman on a series of negotiations in the bazaar that culminate in his marrying a princess and winning a place at court. The apes never re-appear, and the only point, if there is one at all, seems to be that even the lowliest person can move up in the world if he remains open to irrational interventions in his mediocre life.

The stories in the *Thousand and One Nights*, though undeniably entertaining, have essentially no religious content whatsoever, apart from the obligatory sprinkling of pious utterances and oaths to the Prophet. The purpose of such tales is nothing more than titillation and wish-fulfillment. Animals, when and where they appear, are merely narrative instruments, injecting a bit of magic and exoticism into already unbelievable situations. As such, these stories shed very little light on Muslim notions about actual animals, and any influence in shaping (as opposed to merely mirroring) the attitudes of Muslims toward the various species mentioned in the stories is hard to discern.

Animals in Persian Literature

With Persian superseding Arabic as the language of popular Muslim literature throughout the Islamic East beginning in the tenth century, new animal figures became prominent, especially the nightingale who represents the unrequited lover, and a fabulous mythical bird called the Simorgh. The menagerie of animal symbols expanded still further as Islam took root in the Indian subcontinent from the eleventh century onward, incorporating all manner of exotic birds, elephants, monkeys, and other creatures.

THE *PARROT BOOK*

Kalila and Dimna, the *Thousand and One Nights*, and other similar works of popular literature cannot truly be said to have an "author" as such, since the stories they contain are the products of long oral traditions. (This is true of epics such as the *Iliad* and the *Odyssey*, the Icelandic sagas, the *Book of Kings*, and the *Mahabharata* and the *Ramayana*, among others.) In certain cases, however – Aesop's fables come to mind – the name of a particular compiler comes to be irrevocably associated with a particular collection. Such is the case with the fourteenth-century work known as the *Parrot Book* (*Tūtī-nāma*), compiled by Zia al-din Nakhshabi (d. 1350), a Persian-speaker of Central Asian origin who lived in the north Indian city of Badaun not far from Delhi.

Like the tales in *Kalila and Dimna*, the *Parrot Book* stories are said to have originated in India, and to have come to Nakhshabi in the form of a Persian translation which he then revised and supplemented with quotations from the Qur'an and Persian literature. Indeed, ancient Sanskrit texts (including the *Panchatantra*, the *Śukasaptati* and others) seem to be the major source for this genre of literature. As the translator of the *Parrot Book* notes, such works were mainly intended as entertainment for the ruling classes, and animal characters were often used as a way of describing social injustice and oppression.[10]

Nakhshabi's *Parrot Book* consists of the usual "Russian doll" arrangement of tales within tales, told against the backdrop of a marital drama. A traveling businessman leaves at home his young wife, who (naturally!) is tempted to infidelity during his absence. She confides in their pet myna bird, who tries to dissuade her from her illicit desires, but the sexually frustrated wife refuses to listen and cruelly kills the bird. Next she turns to their pet parrot, who, being somewhat more clever than the myna, tries to avoid the latter's fate by responding more subtly, through stories.

Similar to the plot in the *Thousand and One Nights* where Shahrzad keeps her husband from committing his crimes by enthralling him with tales until dawn, the parrot prevents its mistress from going out to visit her lover by recounting tales (mainly of other women's immoral behavior) through the night. This goes on for fifty-two nights, until the husband finally returns. Nakhshabi's own views on unfaithful women are expressed in the following verse, which he interjects on two separate occasions:

O Nakhshabi, an immoral woman deserves the sword
Respect is due to any man who kills an unfaithful wife
If such a disloyal woman dies, who will grieve for her?
It is best that a heavy sword deprive her of her life.[11]

Once again, we are clearly dealing with morals that really have to do with humans, and from a decidedly male (not to say misogynistic) point of view. Animals exist as stand-ins or fly-on-the-wall observers of human behavior, rather than as beings in their own right.

The narrator of the *Parrot Book* is an impossibly human-like parrot who can recite the Qur'an and is valued at a thousand dinars. When the young merchant scoffs at the notion that a mere bird can merit such a prize, the parrot himself replies:

Oh, young man, how can you know my value, and how can you determine my worth? Though I may be a handful of feathers, because of the extent of my knowledge, I triumph over all. Theologians are amazed at my eloquence, and men of great wisdom are astonished at my ability in debating. I am not a messenger of God though I am wearing green [the color of the Prophet]. I am not a *houri* [heavenly maiden] with a cloak over my shoulder. I am not a zealot, but I can travel as a devout servant of God. I am religious, but I have wings. I am not a king, but I am worthy of a high position. I am not a scribe, but I am eloquent. Praise be to God, I am an excellent speaker.[12]

Though it is not hard to imagine some actual Muslim parrot-owner training his bird to recite the Qur'an, the description of this particular parrot is obviously exaggerated. His role perhaps mimics that of a faithful servant (who would have had to be a eunuch under the circumstances), but of course parrots are more colorful.

The first tale told by the parrot narrator is of a parrot very like himself, forced to play the role of mediator in a dysfunctional human marriage. In a status-conscious traditional society with little means for upward mobility, the reversal of power relationships can be a powerful literary tool, whether it be lower-class humans miraculously becoming royalty, as in certain *Thousand and One Nights* stories, or the orchestration of human events by animals in the *Parrot Book*.

Another tale seems to offer a similar reversal, that of a dog who "was accorded more esteem than anyone in the village." This is no ordinary dog, however: it is the dog of Layla, the young beauty for love of whom the madman Majnun (literally, "Madman") condemned himself to a life of solitude in the desert. If the dog possesses more importance than most humans, it is nevertheless from a human, his mistress Layla, that this importance derives. Once again, the elevation of a lowly animal to an exalted station seems to be primarily a narrative device.

Occasionally animal examples are used to illustrate the "laws of nature," to which humans too are presumably bound. For example, in the fifth night's story, a mother parrot instructs her young, saying:

What friendship can there be between birds and wild beasts, and what compatibility can exist between wild animals and parrots? Friendship, trust, or affection established between opposing species is never wise, for that type of friendship never brings happiness. What congeniality can exist between a donkey and a ring-dove, and what benefits can an elephant derive from being close to a gnat?[13]

The message here corresponds neither to interspecies relations in nature nor to human communities, where cooperation between differing communities is vital to the survival of all. Rather, it would appear to be a somewhat feeble attempt to justify xenophobia and class divisions.

The Story of the Lion and the Cat (the Fifteenth Night) is an example of political allegory illustrating the strategies of those who wish to remain in royal service by keeping themselves indispensable. The lion (who is, as always, the King) has a mouse problem, and hires the cat to handle it. The cat knows he will hold onto his job only as long as he allows some mice to survive; one night, however, his overzealous son exterminates all the mice and, sure enough, once the lion realizes mice are no longer a problem, he fires the cat.[14] Real lions and cats, needless to say, have no such relationship.

We have already seen that what appear to be animals can sometimes be other beings – such as humans or genies – which have taken animal form. In the story of the eighteenth night, Moses saves a pigeon about to be eaten by an eagle, offering the eagle a pigeon's weight of his own flesh in exchange. It turns out the birds are actually the angels Michael and Gabriel, come to test his generosity and selflessness.[15] A story such as this is more likely intended to highlight the exceptional qualities of an ancient prophet than to recommend that anyone actually offer his own flesh to birds.

An interesting twist on the Moses episode occurs in the story of the thirtieth night, when a nasty woman thrown out of the house by her husband finds herself in the jungle in danger of being eaten by a leopard. Like Moses, she offers herself as a sacrificial meal, but in her case it is for the purpose of tricking the leopard. In the *Parrot Book* all women are conniving liars, and in this story the hungry leopard is merely her buffoon.

The irremediable infidelity and deceitfulness of women is the thematic thread tying together the parrot's fifty-two stories, not the lives or qualities of the many animals that adorn the tales. The parrot narrator, having won his freedom by informing on his mistress, announces that if all humans are like her he wants nothing to do with them. The woman's husband, after killing her to save his honor, decides the same and ends his days as a pious hermit.

SUFI LITERATURE

Muslim mystics made use of the literary and popular symbols of their times, principally roses and wine, but which included references to animals as well. Again, in most cases such references were symbolic rather than descriptive, using stereotyped animal traits as commentaries on human character and behavior. Moreover, among the Sufis a central notion, and a highly negative one, was that of the "animal self" (*nafs*), the source of all the baser instincts which it is the mystic's goal to overcome. This "animal self," often referred to as a "dog," is described through all manner of animal imagery, which can hardly be considered flattering or positive in regard to animals.

The Conference of the Birds

Mystics of all religions have long used birds to symbolize the flight of the soul up to heaven. But, as Ali Asani notes, "no other tradition of mysticism has developed as elaborate a symbolism and imagery related to birds as Sufism."[16] The most popular image is that of the nightingale (*bulbul* in Persian) singing to the rose (*gul*), a metaphor for the lover singing of his hopeless yearning to the Beloved (identified in the mystic tradition as God). While bird imagery appears in the work of virtually every Sufi poet, the best-known example is surely *The Conference of the Birds* (*Mantiq al-tayr*) by Farid al-din 'Attar (ca. 1130–ca. 1229), an epic poem of nearly five thousand couplets which was completed in 1177.

The gist of the poem is that the birds of the world have gathered together and decided they need a king. One of them, the hoopoe, insists that they have a king already, the Simorgh (a magical bird from ancient Iranian mythology), but that they must find him. The hoopoe takes charge and tries to motivate a large group of birds to set off in search of their rightful leader and guide, but many of them find excuses not to come. Of those that do eventually embark upon the quest, many are not up to the challenge and fall by the wayside. In the end only thirty birds remain, and the resulting Persian pun, "thirty (*si*) birds (*morgh*)" indicates that they themselves are that "Simorgh" which they have been seeking all along.

At each stage of the journey individual birds raise their objections, ask their questions, and look for excuses to beg off the project. These delays serve as a pretext for the hoopoe (a rather transparent stand-in for 'Attar himself) to offer his words of wisdom and insight to his fellow seekers. In most cases the hoopoe's stories are explicitly about humans, though they too are often metaphors (for example, the King as a representation of God). In others animal images are used, but always for a didactic purpose, as in the story of the spider, which is presumably a commentary on verse 29:41 in the Qur'an:

> You've seen an active spider work – he seems
> To spend his life in self-communing dreams
> In fact the web he spins is evidence
> That he's endowed with some far-sighted sense
> He drapes a corner with his cunning snare
> And waits until a fly's entangled there
> Then dashes out and sucks the meager blood
> Of his bewildered, buzzing, dying food
> He'll dry the carcass then, and live off it
> For days, consuming bit by tasty bit
> Until the owner of the house one day
> Will reach up casually to knock away
> The cunning spider's home – and with her broom
> She clears both fly and spider from the room
> Such is the world, and one who feeds there is
> A fly trapped by that spider's subtleties.[17]

The punch line betrays the real purpose of the tale, which is to make a point about the futility and insignificance of the worldly preoccupations of humans. As the poem's English translator, Dick Davis, notes, "Though the stories are ostensibly told by the hoopoe to birds they are in reality told by Attar to men, and the admonitions in them are almost always addressed to humanity, 'Attar's real audience, rather than to the hoopoe's fictitious avian audience."[18]

Jalal al-din Rumi

Jalal al-din Rumi (1207–1273), founder of the Mevlevi Sufi order (the "Whirling Dervishes") is one of the best-known mystics of all time, and modern renditions of his verse have made him the best-selling poet in English today. His vast thirteenth-century poetic opus, the *Mathnawī al-ma'anawī*, is sometimes referred to as "the Qur'an in Persian," so great has been its influence and popularity in Muslim societies. Rumi's poetry abounds in animal images, particularly the kind of bird imagery referred to above. For Rumi, the nightingale represents the perfect lover:

> For Heaven's sake don't talk about the rose!
> Talk about the nightingale who is separated from his rose![19]

The falcon also appears frequently in Rumi's work, as a metaphor for the soul which returns to God. This image plays on the Persian pun on the word *bāz*, which means both "falcon" and "come back":

> How should the falcon (*bāz*) not fly from the hunt towards its King
> When it hears the news "Return!" (*bāz āyad!*) when the drum is beaten?[20]

In most other cases Rumi uses animal characters to represent human traits, such as a donkey for stubbornness. Sometimes, however, animals serve as a contrast for human weaknesses, as when Rumi emphasizes the exemplary faith of non-human animals in their Creator:

> The dove on the tree is uttering thanks to God, though her food is not yet ready.
> The nightingale is singing glory to God, saying, "I rely on Thee for my daily bread, O Thou who answerest prayer."
> . . .
> You may take every animal from the gnat to the elephant: they have all become God's dependents . . .
> [While] these griefs within our breasts arise from the vapor and dust of our existence and vain desire.[21]

According to Rumi, non-human animals even excel humans in some qualities, particularly that of the loving devotion to which Sufis aspire:

> Wolf and bear and lion know what love is:
> He that is blind to love is inferior to a dog!
> If the dog had not a vein of love,

How should the dog of the Cave have sought to win the
  heart of the Seven Sleepers?[22]
You have not smelt the heart in your own kind:
How should you smell the heart in wolf and sheep?[23]

On the other hand, Rumi's vision of the mystic quest follows
Aristotle's "great chain of being," in which the soul travels
upward from an inorganic state to vegetable to animal to that of
a human, before ultimately becoming lost in its Creator:

I died to the inorganic state and became endowed with
  growth
And [then] I died to [vegetable] growth and attained the
  animal.
I died from animality and became Adam [man]: why then
  should I fear?
When have I become less for dying?[24]

So it would seem that even if non-human animals possess laudable qualities, the value of these lies mainly in their instructive
potential for humans, who are nevertheless a stage above them in
the cosmic hierarchy.

Other Sufi Sources

Animals can be a means by which God allows Muslims to earn
his pleasure through their compassionate acts. Similar to the
hadith about the thirsty dog mentioned in chapter one, the well-
known Iraqi Sufi Abu Bakr Dulaf al-Shibli (d. 945) is said to have
told about a dream in which a deceased friend appeared to him.
The friend explained that despite a lifetime of prayers, fasting
and devotion, the reason he had been granted paradise was
because he once rescued a cat from the cold.[25]

Other Sufi stories offer lessons about compassion and renunci-
ation, using the theme of abstention from killing animals for meat.
One such story, from a hagiography compiled by 'Attar, features
the eighth-century female Muslim mystic Rabi'a of Basra:

Rabi'a had gone up on a mountain. Wild goats and
gazelles gathered around, gazing upon her. Suddenly,

Hasan Basri [another well-known early Muslim mystic] appeared. All the animals shied away. When Hasan saw that, he was perplexed and said, "Rabi'a, why do they shy away from me when they were so intimate with you?" Rabi'a said, "What did you eat today?" "Soup." "You ate their lard. How would they not shy away from you?"[26]

'Abd al-Karim al-Qushayri (d. 1074 CE) tells a similar story about the early Sufi Ibrahim ibn Adham, who, it is said, liked to go hunting. One day, as he was pursuing an antelope, he heard a voice asking him, "O Ibrahim, is it for this that We have created you?" Immediately he got down from his horse, gave his fine clothes to a shepherd in exchange for a wool tunic, and assumed the life of a wandering dervish.[27]

Like ascetics in other traditions, Muslims who chose to devote their lives to contemplation often did so in nature, away from the distractions of human society. The definition of "wilderness" (Persian *biābān*), to which the ideal ascetic would retreat, generally includes the presence of wild animals. For example, the Indian saint Baba Farid is said to have chosen to live in a place where "snakes and animals were to be found everywhere."[28] This often led to an increased appreciation for the marvels of God's creation, and in some cases to a greater affection for animals. The fourteenth-century Indian Sufi Shaykh Ahmad of Ahmedabad is described in his hagiography as being a great animal lover, even paying money for injured birds so that he could nurse them back to health.[29]

A number of Sufism's well-known historical figures have been vegetarian. Most stories about Sufi vegetarians originate in South Asia, suggesting possible Hindu or Buddhist influence.[30] On the other hand, a few vegetarian anecdotes also occur among the Sufis of North Africa and the Ottoman world.[31] Generally speaking, however, among the Sufis vegetarianism is seen as a form of spiritual discipline intended to benefit the one who practices it, rather than out of interest for the animals who are spared.

Animals in Art

The tradition of Muslim representational art (as opposed to "Islamic art" strictly speaking, which is non-representational), was most highly developed in Iran and spread from there to India, Turkey, and Central Asia. It is rich with animal themes, especially when illustrating animal stories such as *Kalila and Dimna* and royal hunting scenes, and can be seen in books, carpets, metalwork, ceramics, and rock engravings. Lion figures, associated in the Iranian tradition with monarchy, appear on many public buildings, even sometimes (as in the case of Samarkand's seventeenth-century *Shīr-dār*, or "lion-bearing" seminary) religious ones. Generally speaking, the representational kind of arts that often featured animals are more common in the Iranian-influenced eastern part of the Muslim world than in the Arab west.

Animal figures appear in the work of Muslim artists from as early as the Umayyad period (660–749), which is to say virtually from the beginnings of Islamic civilization. The oldest such examples are icons of political power, such as lions attacking gazelles, which adorned the palaces of some of the Arab elite. Horses were also popular animal images associated with the powerful, with images of prey animals, like deer, no doubt symbolizing the weak. The depiction of zodiac animals, likewise, was a reflection of the ruling class's interest in astrology. The images of this early period were borrowed mainly from Sasanian or Hellenistic models.[32]

By the tenth century animal figures become much more common, especially in jewelry and textiles. With the establishment of the Turkish empires during the following century came increasing influence from Asia, seen notably in the metalwork of the period. Animal motifs, which served a talismanic function in the steppe cultures, became more prevalent on public buildings as well. The fine art of Islamic calligraphy, preferred by purists to representational art, was nevertheless sometimes formed into animal shapes.

Around the same time representational painting of animals increasingly appears in the form of book illustrations. A Persian translation of Ibn Bakhtishu's *Benefits of Animals* done for the Mongol Il-Khan ruler Ghazan Khan at the end of the thirteenth century contains ninety-four paintings of mammals, birds, reptiles, insects, and humans, all in vivid natural settings. Illustrated texts, being very expensive to produce, were done exclusively for the elites. They included not only scientific books, but more especially works of popular literature such as *Kalila and Dimna* and the *Parrot Book*.

Animals also figure in the hunting and garden scenes that adorned court histories and heroic works such as the *Book of Kings* (*Shāh-nāma*), the great Iranian poetic epic so loved (and, no doubt, identified with) by Muslim rulers. While some garden and nature scenes are rather idyllic, many of these paintings are extremely graphic in their depiction of bloody violence, of which animals are generally on the receiving end.

The illustrated *Book of Kings* produced in the ateliers of the Iranian Safavid king Tahmasp in the 1520s is acclaimed by art historians as possibly the finest example of Persian book art in all of history.[33] The most delicate and stunning painting of the 258 in the book – and perhaps in the entire miniature painting tradition – depicts the Court of Gayumars, a sort of Zoroastrian Eden-before-the-fall scene, which includes all manner of animals and humans gathered together in a circle of peace and beauty. In Zoroastrian, as in biblical tradition, such harmony unfortunately could not last.

Under the Mughal rulers of India in the sixteenth and seventeenth centuries, Indian artists trained by Iranian masters incorporated local styles and themes in which nature and animal scenes took on a livelier and more realistic quality than in the highly stylized Persian tradition.[34] Mughal court painters, especially Mansur (fl. ca. 1620), went so far as to create highly refined portraits of individual animals, apparently for no other reason than that they found them beautiful subjects for artistic study. A painting of two peafowl by Mansur and another of squirrels in a tree by his colleague Abu'l-Hasan are two of the most delightful animal images in all of Muslim miniature painting. When the Mughal emperor Jahangir received a live zebra as a gift from a visiting embassy, he immediately commissioned Mansur to paint its likeness for inclusion in the royal memoirs.

Though some of the Mughal period animal paintings show a great sensitivity to actual animal subjects and their behavior in genuine natural settings, these are the exception to the rule. For the most part, animals are included in the art of Muslim cultures as components of highly stylized scenes meant to reflect human desires and pleasures. Foremost are garden settings, evoking the Iranian–Islamic notion of paradise, and hunting scenes, depicting the proudest pastime of the ruling classes. In the former case animals are mere ornaments; in the latter, they are primarily the victims of a sort of generalized macho bloodlust.

5

CONTEMPORARY
MUSLIM VIEWS ON
ANIMAL RIGHTS

In recent years a few individual Muslims have given attention to
animal issues as never before. Within this slowly emerging consciousness, extra-Islamic (mainly Western) influences are clearly
present. Growing numbers of Muslim vegetarians and animal
rights activists appear in most cases first to have been converted
to the cause, then sought support and justification for it within
their Islamic tradition. (Indeed, a disproportionate number of
Muslim animal rights activists appear to be Western converts to
Islam.) Some radical reinterpretations have been put forth as a
result, but even so it must be admitted that a preoccupation with
the rights of non-human animals remains firmly outside the
mainstream in Muslim societies around the world today.

For the vast majority of Muslims, a strong stewardship ethic
(_khilāfa_) – in which humans are seen as divinely appointed
"managers" without whom nature cannot survive and has no
meaning – remains the dominant paradigm. The translator of a
widely used collection of hadiths affirms in his introduction to
the section "Duties Towards Animals" that Man [*sic*] is "the
noblest of animals" and that he is "the Lord of Creation."

Acknowledging that animals have the same basic needs as humans, the commentator asserts that "therefore their natural wants should be supplied by men."[1]

The traditional view is well-expressed in a passage from a book by the influential Pakistani revivalist Abu A'la Mawdudi (1903–1979):

> God has honored man with authority over His countless creatures. Everything has been harnessed for him. He has been endowed with the power to subdue them and make them serve His objectives. This superior position gives man an authority over them and he enjoys the right to use them as he likes. But that does not mean that God has given him unbridled liberty. Islam says that all the creation has certain rights upon man. They are: he should not waste them on fruitless ventures nor should he unnecessarily hurt or harm them. When he uses them for his service he should cause them the least possible harm, and should employ the best and least injurious methods of using them.
>
> The law of Islam embodies many injunctions about these rights. For instance, we are allowed to slaughter animals for food and have been forbidden to kill them merely for fun or sport and deprive them of their lives without necessity . . . Similarly, killing an animal by causing continuous pain and injury is considered abominable in Islam. Islam allows the killing of dangerous and venomous animals and beasts of prey only because it values man's life more than theirs. But here too it does not allow their killing by resort to prolonged painful methods.
>
> Regarding the beasts of burden and animals used for riding and transport, Islam distinctly forbids man to keep them hungry, to take hard and intolerable work from them and to beat them cruelly. To catch birds and imprison them in cages without any special purpose is considered abominable. What to say of animals: Islam does not approve even of the useless cutting of trees and bushes. Man can use their fruit and other produce, but he has no right to destroy

them. Vegetables, after all, possess life, but Islam does not allow the waste of even lifeless things; so much so that it disapproves of the wasteful flow of too much water. Its avowed purpose is to avoid waste in every conceivable form and to make the best use of all resources – living and lifeless.[2]

Another contemporary Muslim thinker, 'Uthman 'Abd al-Rahman Llewellyn, takes note of how modern farming methods intensify the moral dimension of killing to ensure our own survival:

When all the losses of sentient life associated with farming and ranching are taken into account, including not only animals that are slaughtered, but also their parasites, and all the insect, bird, and mammal pests [*sic*] that must be killed to raise a viable crop, all the microscopic creatures in the soil that are crushed by ploughing or trampling, and all the lives affected by the biological and chemical controls that we use, we cannot escape the fact that our lives involve the death of an appalling amount of sentient life. Of course we are morally bound to minimize this suffering and destruction. But we must recognize that agriculture is at least as costly in terms of life and suffering – and environmental impact – as the raising and harvesting of livestock.

To live in this world we must take from it, for life must feed on life to live. The daily bread and meat from which we draw our strength and build our flesh is at the cost of a myriad of lives. How shall we redeem their killing? If we do not use this strength to give back more than we have taken, then what are we ourselves but parasites? But if, in slaughtering and eating, we take God's name in gratitude and render thanks by building beauty, teaching truth, bringing new life to the land, or striving in His cause, we may transmute our lives into yet more life, and give meaning to their deaths, and sanctify them. Then the selfsame act of slaughter will no more be an act of desecration, but an offering of sacrifice.[3]

Many Muslim scholars today, when asked about animal rights in Islam, are quick to assert that the tradition has always been "animal-friendly" but do not explore the issue beyond the rehearsing of a few scriptural references. Egyptian cleric Yusuf al-Qaradawi's remarks are representative:

> Islam preceded Animal Care Societies by thirteen hundred years and made kindness to animals a part of the faith and cruelty to them a sufficient reason for a person to be thrown into Hell-fire.
>
> The protection of animals' rights found its realization in *shari'a* as represented in legal textbooks. It is really interesting to notice how the idea of animals' rights occupied the minds of medieval Muslim jurists. It is a distinctive characteristic of the *shari'a* that all animals have legal rights which must be enforced by the state.[4]

The contemporary Iranian cleric Hashem Najy Jazayery, in his introduction to a recent collection of references to animals in the collected sayings of the Shi'ite imams, considers that according to Islam "any mistreatment of animals must be counted as a great sin," but goes on to say that "mistreatment of humans and the trammeling of human rights is an even greater sin."[5] Nor does he elaborate on how "mistreatment of animals" is to be defined, beyond the contexts of the eighth- and ninth-century sources in which the main injunctions are not to torture animals and to give them water when they are thirsty.

Thus, the sentiments of modern-day Islamic scholars such as those mentioned above probably represent the most conscientious form of traditional Islamic attitudes toward animals, while remaining nevertheless firmly hierarchical and instrumental. Humans are to make "proper" use of animals and other "resources" – the notion that they might be more than just resources is not really emphasized. Against the backdrop of the established view (though perhaps not when compared to Western animal rights discourse), arguments by such contemporary Islamic animal rights advocates as B. A Masri and Said Nursi seem quite radical.

B. A. Masri

Unquestionably the most prominent contemporary voice in articulating Islamic concern for non-human animals is the late Basheer Ahmad Masri (a.k.a. al-Hafiz al-Masri, 1914–1993), a native of India who spent twenty years as an educator in Africa before moving to England in 1961, where he became imam of the Shah Jehan mosque in Woking. Masri's stated worldview, that "life on this earth is so intertwined as an homogeneous unit that it cannot be disentangled for the melioration of one species at the expense of the other,"[6] could just as easily have come from deep ecology, though Masri himself was no deep ecologist.

Masri introduces his 1987 tract *Islamic Concern for Animals* – a valuable but lamentably hard-to-find work – with the following words:

> Cruelty to animals has existed throughout the ages. It takes various forms and guises, from cockfighting to cat burning, from sheer overloading of beasts of burden to downright neglect and abuse. Animals have died, and are dying, harsh deaths in traps and snares to provide fur coats and ornaments for the wealthy, and they have been hunted throughout the world for the sheer sport and morbid pleasure of man. However, until very recently the acts of cruelty were on a smaller and individual scale. What has changed now is the nature and extent of the cruelty, which is practiced on a much subtler and wider scale. The most alarming aspect of the current streak of cruelty is that it is being justified in the name of human needs and spurious science . . . All this, and much more, is being done to satisfy human needs most of which are non-essential, fanciful, wasteful and for which alternative humane products are readily available.[7]

At first glance, Masri's views on factory farming and animal testing seem to mirror those of today's most committed animal rights activists. He writes, further, that

> To kill animals to satisfy the human thirst for inessentials is a contradiction in terms within the Islamic tradition.

Think of the millions of animals killed, in the name of com-
mercial enterprises, in order to supply a complacent public
with trinkets and products they do not really need. And
why? Because we are too lazy or too self-indulgent to find
substitutes.[8]

Masri takes all the world's institutional religions – implicitly
including Islam – to task for failing to take action against our
abuses of other species. "One seldom hears from their pulpits any
sermons or preaching the world of God about animals or respect
for nature," he remarks. "Perhaps the clerics of our religions are
too busy preparing their respective laities for the Life Hereafter
to spare any thought for the so-called 'dumb beasts' and the ecology which sustains us all."[9]

The complicity of organized religions in the mistreatment of
animals comes, Masri believes, from a selfishly selective interpretation of the notion of divinely appointed stewardship. In the case
of Islam, he points out that certain Qur'anic verses are often used
to justify human superiority by taking them out of context. For
example, one of the verses about stewardship (*khilāfa*), "He it is
Who made you vice-regents on earth" actually concludes, "he
who disavows, the burden of disavowal will be upon him."[10]
Likewise, the verse, "Certainly, We created Man in the best
make," is followed by the warning, "then We reduce him to the
lowest of the low."[11] Masri is emphatic that the stewardship with
which we have been entrusted is conditional, and that it can be
taken away if we abuse it.

One of Masri's great concerns is the cruelties involved in
laboratory testing on animals. He is adamantly opposed to the
kinds of "frivolous" research described by Peter Singer in chapter two of *Animal Liberation*, such as cosmetics testing or
psychological experiments.

Yet Masri does not argue against animal testing as such, only
that it should not result in pain or disfigurement to the animal. He
concedes that it is acceptable "if human beings or other animals
would benefit because of the research."[12] For purposes of determining just what kind of "benefit" would qualify, Masri resorts

to the procedures of Islamic jurisprudence. The legal tradition makes a distinction between vital needs (*masāla zarūriyya*), comfort needs (*masāla hajiyya*), and luxury "needs" (*masāla tahsīniyya*). Only in the case of the first, Masri argues, can the causing of suffering to animals be justified, and then only on the established legal principle that "If two evils conflict, choose the lesser evil to prevent the greater evil." Even so, Masri continues, "experiments on animals are allowed as an exception and as a lesser evil and not as a right."[13] The problem here would seem to be that in Muslim societies as much as in the West, the lines between vital and non-vital needs tend to be arbitrarily drawn.

On the subject of factory farming, Masri is categorical: it is not compatible with Islamic ethics toward animals. He is clearly troubled by the unquestioning way in which Muslim countries have adopted industrial farming practices developed in the West:

> The politicians and economists of those Islamic countries which have started following blindfold in the footsteps of the West should ask themselves a few pertinent questions at this stage – before they get their countries entangled inextricably in the Western system of farming and animal husbandry. Do these animals, upon which man has always depended for his food, have certain basic rights? For instance, the right to the companionship of their own kind, the right to an appropriate diet to keep them in health, and the right to a natural life and painless death? If their Divine Creator gave them legs, is it not a blasphemy to shut them in crates where they are unable to walk? Are we perhaps forcing them back upon their own evolution and becoming more bestial ourselves, unable to know right from wrong?[14]

Masri believes that the imposition of industrial farming in Muslim societies can occur only under a cloud of obscurity. (The same could be said, of course, about factory farming in any society.) It is the role of Islamic scholars, Masri feels, to provide the public with the necessary information and critical perspective:

> Most of such un-Islamic businesses are flourishing in the Islamic countries due to the ignorance of the consumer

public. People do not know how the chickens are being reared and how they are being fed on chemical nutrients to fatten fast and to produce more and more eggs. Fowls and other food animals are no longer creatures of God; they are numbers on their computers. After all, computers can give the breeders up-to-the-minute figures of profit and loss at the touch of a button, while God's reckoning is a long way off in the Hereafter. If only the average, simple and God-fearing Muslim consumers of such food animals knew the gruesome details about the Westernized meat industry in their own Islamic countries, they would become vegetarians rather than eat such sacrilegious meat . . . The least the Muslim *'Ulama'* can do is inform the lay public about how their food is being produced, so that people can – with. knowledge – decide what to do about it.[15]

Himself a lifelong vegetarian, Masri shied away in his published writings from actually advocating a vegetarian diet for Muslims, merely suggesting it is a choice Muslims may wish to make once they know what is really going on. "Some may decide," he writes, "that the products of intensive factory farms are not suitable, both from the religious and the health points of view, and seek more naturally produced eggs and meat; or give up eating meat altogether."[16]

Still, near the end of his treatise Masri allows himself to wonder "why Islam, with all its concern for animals, has allowed its followers to consume their meat and did not ask them to become vegetarian, like some other religions." He just as quickly shelves the question, however, saying merely that we should "accept the fact that Islam has allowed the slaughter of animals for food and see what instructions it gives us to ensure humane slaughter, with as little pain to the victim as possible."[17]

Masri states his position far more strongly in a video he made near the end of his life in 1993. Titled *Creatures of God*, this low-budget, 27-minute film was produced by the same organization that published Masri's two books on animals, the International Association Against Painful Experiments on Animals (IAAPEA) based in Petersfield, England. The format is that of a lecture (or sermon) in Arabic on a bare set, with summarized voice-overs in English, interspersed with cutaway shots of various forms of animal abuse occurring both in Muslim societies and in the West.

Unlike in his books, in this videotaped presentation Masri actually argues that Muslims should consider becoming vegetarians, even to the point where some of his textual interpretations seem stretched. After laying out the conditions of factory farming and citing the familiar hadiths and Qur'anic verses about compassion, he says firmly that "We can no longer avoid the strong Islamic counsel in favor of a vegetarian diet." Later he contends that "Islam teaches us that any killing is a grave sin, and can only be justified if life and limb are in grave danger." This seems an overstated reading of the texts – in any case, Masri then goes on to speak at length about the need for "humane" slaughter, never acknowledging that the very notion itself may be an oxymoron.

Otherwise, the substance of Masri's video sermon is essentially the same as that in his books, but much more strongly put. Whereas emotional pleas are largely absent from Masri's written work, on camera he uses language such as, "The most sickening things are being done to animals in the name of science," "There can be no justification at all in the Islamic tradition for these cruelties," and "If we cannot take the guidance of direct Islamic teachings [on animals], then how can we feel true to other aspects of our faith?"

Masri likens factory farming, laboratory testing, and sport hunting to the pre-Islamic pagan practices of the Arabs, and calls for a new project of animal-rights *ijtihād* in response to modern forms of animal abuse: "Should we not apply Islamic law to the present-day successors of these pagan acts?" He sums up his lecture with the following words:

> If we take as a whole the teaching we find in the Holy Qur'an and the *ahādith* and judge them in their true spirit, no one will deny the fact that Allah requires of us to apply the same moral code to all creatures, including animals, as we apply to our fellow human beings.

Masri's interpretations here are clearly every bit as strong as the most committed animal rights activist could desire. They remain, however, his own interpretations, and while his stature as a member of the *'ulama'* class gives them a certain amount of weight, Masri's views do not seem to reflect the mainstream either among his scholarly peers or in Muslim societies as a whole. Masri's voice is a pioneering one in the domain of Islamic values and animal rights, but it will have to be joined by many others if the attitudes and behaviors of Muslims toward animals is to change.

Said Nursi

The late Turkish Sufi master Bediüzzaman Said Nursi (1877–1960) is heralded by his followers as a model animal-lover.[18] As a result of time spent in prison, where he witnessed the indiscriminate spraying of insecticides, Nursi wrote an entire treatise on the importance of flies.[19] He also claimed to be able, like Solomon, to understand animal languages, as in the following passage:

> . . . one day I looked at the cats; all they were doing was eating, playing, and sleeping. I wondered, how is it these little monsters which perform no duties are known as blessed? Later, I lay down to sleep for the night. I looked; one of the cats had come. It lay against my pillow and put its mouth against my ear, and murmuring: "O Most Compassionate One! O Most Compassionate One!" in the most clear manner, as though refuting in the name of its species the objection and insult which had occurred to me, throwing it in my face. Then this occurred to me: I wonder if this recitation is particular to this cat, or is it general among cats? And is it only an unfair objector like me who hears it, or if anyone listens carefully, can they hear it? The next morning I listened to the other cats; it was not so clear, but to varying degrees they were repeating the same invocation. At first, "O Most Compassionate!" was discernible following their purring. Then gradually their purrings and meowings became the same "O Most Merciful!" It became an unarticulated, eloquent and sorrowful recitation.

They would close their mouths and utter a fine "O Most Compassionate!" I related the story to the brothers who visited me, and they listened carefully as well, and said that they heard it to an extent.[20]

Nursi is said to have shared food with ants, cats, mice, and pigeons, and to have reprimanded a student for killing a lizard, asking him "Did you create it?"[21] One of his teachings is that the universe is fundamentally "clean," and that it is often little-appreciated animal species who are responsible for keeping it that way:

> It is not only the carnivorous cleaners of the seas and the eagles of the land which obey the commands proceeding from that sacred cleansing, but also its cleansing officials which gather up corpses, like worms and ants.[22]

Nursi appears to have belonged to the minority of Muslims who believe that animal souls are eternal. He even suggests that natural carnivores should restrict themselves to eating the flesh of animals that are already dead, and that failure to do so will result in punishment in the hereafter:

> The licit food of carnivorous animals is the flesh of dead animals. The flesh of living animals is unlawful for them. If they eat it, they receive punishment. The hadith which states that "Retaliation shall be made for the hornless sheep on the horned on Resurrection Day" points out that although their bodies perish, among animals whose spirits are immortal there is reward and punishment in a manner appropriate for them in the eternal realm. As a consequence of this it may be said that the flesh of live animals is unlawful for wild animals.[23]

Nursi opposed any killing of animals, even flies:

> ... flies are charged with duties of cleaning away poisonous substances and microbes which breed disease and are invisible to the human eye. They do not transmit microbes; on the contrary, through sucking up and imbibing harmful

microbes they destroy them and cause them to be transformed into different state; they prevent the spread of many
contagious diseases. A sign that they are both health workers and cleansing officials and chemists and that they exhibit
extensive wisdom is the fact that they are extremely numerous. For valuable and beneficial things are multiplied.[24]

Nursi's argument extends to mosquitoes as well:

Mosquitoes and fleas fall upon the turbid blood flowing in
the veins polluted by harmful substances, indeed they are
charged with consuming the polluted blood, so in hot
weather when there is blood surplus to the body's needs,
why should they not be natural cuppers?[25]

Nursi emphasized in his teachings that nature is most importantly
a form of divine revelation, and that the signs of nature (*āyāt*) are
to be read like the signs of written language. He goes so far as to
suggest that Creation is the original form of revelation, upon
which the revealed Qur'an is merely a commentary (*tafsīr*).[26]
Following Nursi's line of reasoning, it could be said that when we
destroy habitats and species, it is like burning the pages of the
divine text by which God makes it possible for us to know Him.

As seen in chapter four, historically speaking Sufism has
shown a greater degree of sensitivity than the legal tradition to the
Qur'anic message about non-human animals being *"muslim"*
(that is, "submitters") and, alongside humans, co-worshippers of
God. This type of sensitivity is evident in the testimony of a contemporary British follower of the Pakistani Naqshbandi shaykh
Sufi Abdullah, who sees pigeons as fellow Sufis:

The people here [that is, South Asian immigrants visiting
Sufi Abdullah's center in Birmingham, England] do the
zikr [a mantra-like chant] all the time. Even when they are
working they do the *zikr*. When I came here the first time,
I insisted that I wanted to do some work. So they gave me
an area to clean. I was cleaning one of the rooms when I
heard someone doing the *zikr* in one of the other rooms.
But when I looked into that room, there was no one there.

But I still kept hearing the *zikr*. Then I looked up and saw
there was a pigeon sitting on the edge of the roof doing the
zikr. I had heard that the pigeons do the *zikr* here.[27]

This impression would seem to be drawing on a long tradition in
Sufism attributing Sufi longing to birds, in which the "coo coo"
of pigeons is understood to be the Persian *"Ku ku?"* ("where is
He? where is He?").

Advocacy on the Internet

In 1998 the animal rights organization People for the Ethical
Treatment of Animals (PETA), responding to requests from its
Muslim members, asked member Irfan Ali Robert Tappan, now
a graduate student in Islamic Studies at the University of Virginia,
to design a website on Islam and vegetarianism. Originally called
IslamVeg.com, the site was eventually expanded to include
Islamic perspectives on animal sacrifice, experimentation, and
the use of animals for entertainment and clothing. The site,
which has since been renamed Islamic Concern for Animals
(IslamicConcern.com), now features articles and postings from
Muslim legal scholars, scientists, doctors, and laypeople. While
PETA continues to provide technical support for the site, Tappan
emphasizes that "PETA maintains no control over the content or
direction of IslamicConcern.com, which is driven entirely by
Muslims, either myself or the other contributors to the site."[28]

The IslamicConcern site provides clarifications on Islamic
sacrifice, Islamic views on vivisection, Islamic arguments for vegetarianism and suggestions for *"halāl* living," Islamic critiques of
the wearing of fur, web-based animal books and other resources
for children, and news items on food and health issues connected
with animals. The site draws heavily on the work of B. A. Masri
(which is hardly surprising, given the paucity of qualified
contemporary Islamic scholars who have chosen to investigate
seriously contemporary animal rights issues), but a number of
*fatwa*s from other scholars on specific issues are featured as
well. There are also postings from Muslim doctors and other
professionals.

One of the most interesting items on IslamicConcern is the following argument against vivisection, taken from a taped lecture by homeopathic physician Hakim Archuletta, who is a convert of Native American origin:

> The torture of animals in the name of medicine. For anyone with any common sense, I mean, we lose track of common sense. Our minds are our biggest enemies. We can rationalize and take conceptually, find a rationale to do the most horrific things. This is the nature of the human being. Our minds can make all kinds of excuses and reasons that we should do something.
>
> But from a very practical, common sense point of view, and from the point of view that allows for the *rahma*, the Mercy of Allah, to be present, the idea that we should have to take monkeys, chimpanzees, inject them with AIDS, inject them with hepatitis, that somehow by doing that we may or may not find something that will help this poor suffering creature to serve us in our arrogance as human beings? We are so far above all the rest of Allah's creation that we can do this? This is big, serious detachment from reality. This is a serious break with common sense. And yet, if you go to medical school, if you are a "scientist," you will buy this. Maybe some of you have gone to school, in universities, and they've convinced you that this is true. *Astaghfirullah*! (God forgive us!)
>
> As Muslims we cannot do that. We cannot torture an animal with the idea that we will find some medicine in the process for us. And that is a denial of the immediacy of Allah's mercy.[29]

Tappan notes an increasing interest on the part of Muslims in finding cruelty-free products, though he states that companies have been slow to seek *halāl* certification for their products, even companies that have actively sought kosher certification. He suggests that such companies are "hurting themselves, especially American companies since Muslim American consumers tend to be highly educated and affluent."[30]

An unexpected positive outcome of the IslamicConcern site came after the terrorist attacks of September 11, 2001 in New York City and Washington D.C. Tappan reports that although IslamicConcern, like other sites devoted to Islamic topics, received a lot of hate mail, many who visited the site looking for reasons to criticize Islam came away instead feeling that "a faith that cares about the 'lowest' of God's creation must also care about human beings."[31]

A number of other Islamic websites now include "Animal Rights in Islam" in their longs lists of topics, with B. A. Masri often being the authority of choice. Another source which turns up repeatedly on different sites is a short treatment excerpted from an otherwise obscure educational pamphlet entitled *Animal Rights and Ecology in Islam*.[32] Discussions on animal issues are now appearing on the chat forums of some of these sites as well. If the internet is any indication of where things are heading, there is every sign that interest in animal rights issues, especially among young Muslims living in the West, is on the rise.

Not a Mainstream View

At the same time it must be acknowledged that the kinds of perspectives outlined above remain well outside the Muslim mainstream. In pushing the limits of Islamic tradition, teachers like Masri and Nursi go further even than any of today's self-proclaimed Islamic environmentalists who have mentioned the rights of non-human animals.[33]

For a majority of Muslims both today and historically, the overriding emphasis is on the general legal principle that "One may not forbid something which Allah has made permissible." With a few notable exceptions, even in the formative years of Islam the overall trend in terms of values and norms was perhaps more towards continuity than radical change.

Even so it may be remarked that the standard conservative view ("allowed unless specifically disallowed") is somewhat ahistorical, given that certain things considered permissible in the time of the Prophet have since been largely determined not to be so, human slavery being a major example. Just as the moral marginalization of human slavery is a relatively modern phenomenon, in the Muslim world as in the West, Islamic modernists may eventually determine, as some Western philosophers have done, that the similarities between human and animal slavery outweigh the differences, and that the enslavement of non-human animals merely to satisfy non-essential human needs is no longer defensible. To date, however, in the broader Muslim world this line of reasoning has yet to see the light of day.

Contemporary Muslim Views on Wildlife Conservation

It is abundantly obvious to anyone with training in the field of biology that human survival depends utterly on the integrity of the complex interdependent systems which make up the Earth's biosphere. If any one part of the system crashes, the rest will be affected, and the system as a whole is necessary for any species community, ours included, to live. Biologists also understand the need for diversity within and among species, since diversity – that is, varied kinds of adaptability and resilience, whether to environmental changes, disease, or other challenges – is the best insurance against total extinction.

Unfortunately, most people do not possess even the most basic understanding of how biological systems work, and this includes many if not most of the world's key decision-makers, educators, and spiritual leaders. The dominant paradigm is still founded on a kind of Cartesian–Newtonian mechanistic worldview in which biological systems are erroneously believed to mimic mechanical ones. But nature is not constructed like a clock, and if a spring or a cog goes bad it is not simply a matter of replacing it with a new one. Natural systems are far more complex, as demonstrated by recent scientific insights like chaos theory (a butterfly flapping its wings in the Caribbean can affect tropical storms in Asia) and quantum physics (in which matter that appears to be solid is understood actually to be mostly empty space).

Though scientists around the world today basically accept the same set of operative rules and assumptions about what constitutes proof in scientific experiments, no amount of consensus among scientists can prevail in influencing policy-making when opposing worldviews remain dominant within the society. One example of this can be seen in the United States of America, where Christian fundamentalism and unbridled corporate capitalism alike (and increasingly in concert) have succeeded in sowing widespread doubt among the general population regarding such scientifically established notions as human-induced catastrophic climate change. In the Muslim world, a similar phenomenon exists in regard to exponential human population growth. While the detrimental impact of uncontrolled human expansion on both natural systems and humans is readily demonstrable, the preference in traditional Muslim societies remains for having as many children as possible, relying on the Qur'an-inspired belief that "Allah will provide."[34]

In short, anti-scientific social policy is possible only in the presence of longstanding interpretations that make opposing claims. It is vitally important, therefore, to keep traditions open to the possibility of re-interpretation in light of new data. In former times most humans lived in environments where wildlife and natural resources were so abundant so as to appear inexhaustible. Around the world today most of us continue to live as if this were still the case. Clearly, our received views of the world and how it works have not kept pace with the skyrocketing impact of our activities, or with scientists' understanding of that impact.

Among the major universal religious traditions, Islam possesses perhaps the greatest sensitivity to the value of natural resources and the need to preserve them. This may be due in part to the fact that Islam arose in one of the world's harshest environments. It is therefore somewhat ironic that among all the Muslim societies around the planet today, it is on the Arabian Peninsula that waste and plundering of water and soil are most egregious, an indication that the greed and carelessness fostered by untold wealth have outweighed the principles laid down in the Qur'an.

It is also true historically that some negative and harmful attitudes toward many animal species have existed among

Muslims. This is often due to selective or overzealous interpretations of the tradition's teachings. For example, a respected commentator on one of the most popular hadith collections, the *Mishkāt al-masābih*, writes in introducing the section on "Injurious Animals" that "ferocious beasts . . . should be killed wherever they are found," noting that "there are no exceptions in this class."[35] Applying such an interpretation to practice would certainly lead to the extermination of many species.

A high proportion of today's educated Muslims are scientists. There exists a sizeable literature making the case that, unlike in post-enlightenment Western culture, in Islam there is no conflict between religion and science, but that in fact the two reinforce each other.[36] Thus, while concepts such as "biodiversity" and "species extinction" were not articulated as such when the Qur'an was revealed in the seventh century, contemporary Muslims concerned with wildlife have sought to find the seeds of modern scientific understanding in the Qur'anic revelation. They are able to do so, of course, only by making interpretive claims, and these can always be contested by those with opposing agendas.

Nevertheless, a growing number of Muslim scientists are arguing for a normative, "ecological" interpretation of Islam based on a reading of traditional sources informed by modern scientific knowledge. H. S. A. Yahya, an Indian Muslim ornithologist, writes in his recent book *[The] Importance of Wildlife Conservation from [An] Islamic Perspective*:

> Observing nature's marvel, diversity of species and systems, all provide an excellent refreshing moment and solace in one's life. The fabric of lives of men, women, plants, animals, and other, inanimate objects are very intricately linked. Any imbalance will be disastrous, and would be a deviation from the chosen path of the believers.[37]

Would that all believers had "chosen" the same path as conservationists like Yahya! Unfortunately such interpretations are still rare, whereas the worldviews of most Muslims, like those of other faiths, remain rooted in anthropocentric values and in the obsolete conditions of the past.

Muslim conservationist 'Uthman Llewellyn highlights the fact that in light of the dramatically increased human impact on natural systems, new and expanded interpretations of traditional norms are needed. "In the past," he writes, "most wild populations were little affected by the acts of human beings. Now, their welfare and survival are increasingly, sometimes utterly, dependent on acts of humanity." Citing the Sunni jurist al-Mughni's argument that the legal status of animals is analogous to that of slaves, Llewellyn proposes that their rights should be defended in Islamic courts.[38] There would seem to be more of a basis for this kind of protection in Islamic law than in the legal systems of the West, though to date this potential has not been put into practice.

Iranian–American philosopher Seyyed Hossein Nasr, referring to the Qur'anic verses which state that "all creation praises God,"[39] notes that "In destroying a species, we are in reality silencing a whole class of God's worshippers." From an Islamic point of view, it would be hard to find a more compelling argument for conservation.[40]

6

TOWARDS AN ISLAMIC VEGETARIANISM

Virtually all of the world's 1.2 billion Muslims eat meat, in most cases as often as they can possibly afford to. Distributing meat is also one of the most commonly practiced forms of charity, and a hungry indigent is as likely as a well-to-do dinner guest to feel cheated and insulted if meat is not offered. Muslims, like most people, take the practice of meat-eating to be a given, a fact of nature that need not be questioned. Moreover, as has been seen in this book, the religious tradition appears explicitly to sanction it.

The Qur'an has usually been interpreted as allowing the eating of meat, as in the verse which reads:

> O you who have attained to faith! Be true to your covenants! Lawful to you is every beast that feeds on plants, save what is mentioned to you [hereinafter]: but you are not allowed to hunt while you are in a state of pilgrimage. Behold, God ordains in accordance with his will.[1]

Muslims have perceived a similar permission in the following verse:

> Say: In all that has been revealed unto me, I do not find anything forbidden to eat, if one wants to eat thereof,

unless it be carrion, or blood poured forth, or the flesh
of swine – for that, behold, is loathsome – or a sinful
offering over which any name other than God's has been
invoked. But if one is driven by necessity – neither coveting
it nor exceeding his immediate need – then [know that],
behold, thy Sustainer is much-forgiving, a dispenser of
grace.[2]

The pre-Islamic Arabs, most of whom lived a pastoral-nomadic
existence in a harsh desert climate, were a meat-eating culture by
necessity; in such an environment, a vegetarian diet would have
been challenging to say the least. The Qur'an does not lay down
any such burden, and it seems natural enough that the Arabs
saw nothing in the divine revelation to desist from meat-eating.
As Islamic civilization spread into Asia beginning in the eighth
century, tensions with Buddhists and Hindus – seen as idol-
worshipping infidels – provided Muslims with a further "guilt by
association" argument against vegetarianism.

Ethical questions surrounding the use of animals for food are
not raised in the legal literature of classical Islam, and even today
any serious discourse on the viability of an "Islamic" vegetarianism is difficult to find. In his commentary on the English translation of one of the most widely used hadith collections, the
Mishkāt al-masābih, the Islamic legal scholar Fazlul Karim (an
Indian Muslim and former judge under the British) defends the
eating of meat in the strongest terms:

> . . . it is impossible for man to live without destroying ani-
> mals and animal life. Then again, meat is one of the princi-
> pal foods in cold countries. If they live on vegetables alone,
> they would live cold like dead men. Thirdly, those nations
> that are carnivorous are more brave and courageous than
> those who are herbivorous. This applies in case of animals
> also. The carnivorous animals are more ferocious than
> herbivorous animals. So, to pluck up the virtue of courage
> and bravery, meat is essentially necessary. Fourthly, all the
> religious personalities partook of meat and gave sanction
> to use it as human food. All these show that sacrifice of

animals in some form or other is daily done in our food and there is no escape out of it.[3]

In a similar spirit, the highly influential Indian jurist Ali Ashraf Thanvi, in a recent treatise titled "Animal's Rights in Islam," likens animal slaughter to capital punishment of human criminals:

> Allah has allowed slaughtering animals in the larger interests of mankind. One should not mistake it for an inhuman act. In the same vein, capital punishment for a convict of certain categories has been prescribed in that it ensures the well-being of the human society at large. Both slaughtering and capital punishment are to be taken in the same spirit.[4]

It is difficult to see how the killing of livestock could be "taken in the same spirit" as the execution of criminals, given that the animals in question have committed no crime, but this inconsistency is not addressed by Thanvi.

Popular Islamic lecturer Zakir Naik is another outspoken Muslim opponent of vegetarianism. According to his reasoning, plants feel pain so killing them is morally equivalent to killing animals. This point, if true, might constitute an argument for fruitarianism, but it is hard to see how it supports the morality of eating meat, and in any case there is so far no compelling evidence that plants do feel pain.[5]

In arguing against vegetarianism the Islamic legal scholar Mawil Izzi Dien has gone so far as to assert the following:

> According to Islamic Law there are no grounds upon which one can argue that animals should not be killed for food. The Islamic legal opinion on this issue is based on clear Qur'anic verses. Muslims are not only prohibited from eating certain food, but also may not choose to prohibit themselves food that is allowed by Islam. Accordingly vegetarianism is not permitted unless on grounds such as unavailability or medical necessity. Vegetarianism is not allowed under the pretext of giving priority to the interest of animals because such decisions are God's prerogative.[6]

In other words, according to Izzi Dien, not only is there no such thing as Islamic vegetarianism, but to be a vegetarian is un-Islamic! This might sound like a bizarre interpretation, but the tension for Muslims is apparently a real one. In fact, the main purpose of the IslamicConcern website supported by PETA was originally to help Muslim vegetarians deal with just this prejudice. As the website's founder, Robert Tappan, relates:

> . . . the major issue we tried to tackle was the permissibility of Muslims to be vegetarian or vegan. While we knew of many Muslims who already did eat this way, they faced a great deal of criticism from their coreligionists about their dietary choices. Our first task then was to show that vegetarianism and veganism are acceptable choices for a Muslim, as well as reasons why a Muslim might choose to change their diet in this way (i.e. human health concerns, environmental concerns, and cruelty to animals concerns, all important issues for Muslims), and what sorts of foods could be substituted for Muslims making the switch.[7]

Thus, while Tappan notes that the website initially received much negative feedback from Muslims, for Muslim vegetarians its most useful service was that it provided a number of *fatwa*s on the "permissibility" of vegetarianism.

The list of experts includes such well-known and widely followed figures as Hamza Yusuf, Ibrahim Desai, Sayyid Fadhlullah, Muzammil Siddiqi, M. S. Al-Munajjid – even Iranian Supreme Leader Ayatollah Ali Khamene'i. None of these legal luminaries offers any explicit critique of modern meat-production techniques, or recommends vegetarianism, although a few opine that eating "too much" meat is "reprehensible" (*makrūh*). Many of the respondents emphasize the principle that "meat is allowed, and therefore cannot be disallowed." Shaykh Al-Munajjid cautions the questioner that he can abstain from meat if he wishes to out of personal revulsion, but should not do it as a religious act, for that is what "the Brahmins and monks do."[8]

Tappan, assessing the impact of the IslamicConcern website on Muslims, states that "While resistance to accepting the permissibility of vegetarianism still persists, it is much lower than before, and reference to our list of *fatwa*s seems to convince the majority of doubters."[9] This observation would seem to support the view that in addressing animal rights, as indeed any other contemporary issue, Muslim attitudes are unlikely to undergo any widespread major shift without the support of the *'ulama'*. Evidence of this may be seen in the refusal in 2003 of the Qatar-based television station Al-Jazeera to air an advertisement against animal cruelty prepared by PETA. Ironically, this station, known for regularly broadcasting scenes of war, found the slaughterhouse images in the PETA ad to be "too graphic."[10]

Despite the clear mistrust toward vegetarianism which can be found within the contemporary Islamic mainstream, in actual fact a vegetarianism practiced out of Islamic piety is nothing new. Throughout history numerous Muslims have abstained from meat for spiritual reasons. Often, however, they were ridiculed for their dietary choices, just like vegetarians today. An early female Sufi, Zaynab, is said to have been persecuted for her refusal to eat meat.[11] The eleventh-century Syrian poet al-Ma'arri, mentioned in earlier chapters, became a vegan late in life out of asceticism, but he too was condemned for showing "excessive" compassion to non-human creatures. More recently, Paula Rahima Robinson writes that "When I became a Muslim almost five years ago, I never anticipated the consternation that my vegetarianism would cause . . ."[12]

Contemporary Islamic environmentalists are generally dismissive of vegetarianism. Ali Ahmad, a Nigerian Muslim scholar of environmental law, has this to say:

> Laudable as vegetarianism is, it constitutes an insignificant effort at reducing other innate human urges for consumption and general resource utilization that have been the bane of degradation of the environment. An ideal or ascetic lifestyle that adopts modest consumption of all resources will have greater impact. The argument that killing some specific animals *for the purpose of eating* amounts to cruelty is arbitrary.[13]

Even Ahmad's initial remark that vegetarianism is "laudable" goes beyond what most Muslims today would accept. When I submitted an earlier draft of this chapter to a high-profile Islamic studies journal in 2000, an anonymous reviewer urged the editors in the strongest terms to reject it, on the basis of nothing more than his opinion that the topic itself was unworthy of scholarly attention (although he did suggest that it might make an interesting newspaper article).[14] Such prejudices are, of course, all too familiar to those working in the field of animal rights, whatever the cultural context.[15]

Nevertheless, there is increasing evidence that a specifically Islamic vegetarianism has begun to articulate itself, albeit somewhat timidly.

Islamic Vegetarianism on the Rise

While to date no recognized Muslim legal scholar has argued (in print at least) that the permissibility of meat-eating should be reconsidered, increasing numbers of lay-Muslim vegetarians are making their views known, especially over the internet. A number of postings suggest that the Prophet Muhammad, though an occasional eater of meat, kept mainly to a vegetarian diet.

Muslim doctors are recognizing the benefits of a vegetarian diet for human health. For example, Dr. Shahid Athar of Indiana University Medical School states that, "There is no doubt that a vegetarian diet is healthier and beneficial to health in lowering weight, blood pressure, cholesterol, and blood sugar. Our Prophet was mostly vegetarian."[16] Dr. Moneim A. Fadali, author of *Animal Experimentation: A Harvest of Shame*, writes

> Islam, a religion of compassion and moderation, acknowledges animals' rights and emphasizes humans' responsibility for their welfare. A vegan vegetarian diet is healthful, promotes mental and physical well-being, and is cruelty-free. It does not include animal parts or products such as eggs and dairy products. I urge every Muslim and non-Muslim to become a vegan vegetarian.[17]

In 2001 a Muslim reporter, Sunny Aslam, published a feature story in *USA Today* on the benefits of vegetarianism.[18] UK-based Muslim writer Rafeeque Ahmed argues in a self-published pamphlet that humans were "created by Allah to be vegan."[19] Ghazala Anwar, a professor of Islamic Studies at the University of Canterbury in New Zealand, notes that

> God is *Rahmān* and *Rahīm*, the most compassionate and merciful. The one with true Islam draws close to God by inculcating God's qualities of compassion and mercy, thus a true Muslim is one who honors, sustains, and protects the lives of creatures of God and does not kill them for her own food.[20]

In my Islam and Nature seminar several years ago, a vegetarian Muslim student from Bangla Desh, Sharmeen Qudrot, made an observation that I have not heard anywhere else: that since the Qur'an prohibits the consumption of blood, and given that it is impossible to remove all traces of blood from animal flesh, it might be argued that God actually doesn't want us to eat flesh at all. Her argument seeks out the *spirit* of the prohibition on eating blood. The Islamic legal tradition, meanwhile, has sought merely the *letter* of the law, rationalizing that because of the impossibility of removing blood from an animal's muscle tissue, God must have intended only that we abstain from the blood in the veins (which must be drained prior to eating). This qualification is merely the jurists' interpretation; in most of the relevant verses the Qur'an simply prohibits the consumption of blood, period.[21]

In just the past few years, vegetarian and animal rights societies have begun to appear all over the Muslim world, from Egypt, Jordan, and Syria to Turkey, Iran, Pakistan, Malaysia, and Indonesia, as well as among Muslims in the US and the UK.[22] In Turkey, which has several national vegetarian organizations, an old Istanbul neighborhood known as "Non-meat-eater" (Etyemecz) derives its name from the vegetarian practices of a Sufi sect.[23] Iran has at least one registered vegetarian society, the Sana and Shafa Vegetarians' Association, based in Tehran.[24] A vegetarian restaurant in the center of the Iranian capital serves a mixture of Western and Indian food, and has been doing very well. (I have eaten there myself, and the food is quite good.) There is now a Muslim branch of the International Vegetarian Union (IVU) in the UK.

Internet chat-rooms, both Muslim and vegetarian, have begun to see lively debates on vegetarianism and Islam. The following exchanges are taken from the October 1, 2003 posting of vegblog.com:

Islam and Vegetarianism: An interesting dichotomy:

Muslims shouldn't be vegetarian
First of all, it should be clear that one should not think that it is better to abstain from eating meat, that doing so will be rewarded, or that being a vegetarian is closer to Allah than not, and so on. It is not permitted to draw closer to Allah in this way.

v.s.

Muslims can and should be vegetarian
Vegetarianism is *halāl*.
Meat is not compulsory.
Any food is permissible provided it is not harmful.
Muslims are free to eat whatever they want provided it is *halāl*.

Comments

Islam is the middle way . . . it does not shy away from the natural nor does it wallow in the artificial.
The vehement opposition of some Islamic authorities to vegetarianism as a concept is a reflection of Islam's aversion to sentimentalism.
Meat of certain kinds is without doubt permissible in Islam . . . what people object to is people making an appeal for vegetarianism based on a sentimental view of killing animals which they mistakenly believe does not befit a merciful god.
Some Islamic authorities opposed vegetarianism, because the particular perspective from which it was advocated expressed a particular perception of God which is contrary

to how He is ordinarily perceived in the Islamic tradition. Allah in the Islamic tradition is not reduced to some glib god light and love . . . He is also the Wrathful, the Avenger and the Misguider.

Whilst Allah's loving mercy precedes His wrath . . . His wrath is in fact relative and thus illusionary; the fact is in the material world, the illusion of injustice has to manifest itself in order that the higher principle of mercy can be expressed itself in a hidden way in a higher realm.

Having said that, if we look at the Islamic guidelines regarding the treatment of animals, the abuse of animals under the modern factory system is certainly *harām* . . . The middle way would thus be to refrain from eating meat that has been cultivated under such exploitative circumstances and for Muslims to create pressure groups that can create provisions by which we can ensure the meat we buy is ritualistically as well as ethically *halāl*.

What is indeed important is that Muslims need to contribute greater in the realm of alternative health and vegan/vegetarianism rather than perceiving as an issue for the new age.

Posted by: ahmed on November 10, 2003 07:35 AM

I believe that Mohammed, pbuh, was a vegetarian; it helps, somehow, to see things differently when one avoids the consumption of flesh. Watch the effect.

Posted by: bustani on March 21, 2004 05:26 PM

I'm not a Muslim nor an expert on Islam. But I used to have a coworker who was from Malaysia. He was older and very traditional. He was a very strict Muslim and he was a vegetarian. When I asked him about his vegetarianism, he said that his religion – Islam – required him to be. He seemed like the kind of person who blindly follows whatever scripture they choose to follow. Therefore, I don't think his vegetarianism was of his own interpretation of Islam. I have never encountered a Muslim like him before, but I'm wondering if some branches of Islam do preach vegetarianism. One thing I do know about Islam is that

like any other religion, it mutated depending on a culture
that adapted it and it often appropriated certain local customs and cultural ideals in order to win new converts.
Thus there are Muslims in some parts of Africa who do
things that no Muslims anywhere would ever do, etc. It
would be interesting to find out if some "denominations"
of Islam do advocate vegetarianism.

Posted by: wes hurley on April 28, 2004 10:14 PM

The first link doesn't say vegetarianism is not allowed – it
says one should not forbid oneself what is permitted in
Islam; however, if not eating meat is just a matter of preference it is ok. Also, I think Muhammad (PBUH) wasn't a
vegetarian as he was noted to eat meat on Eid. Personally,
I eat a mostly vegetarian diet. I am more of a social meat
eater (i.e, about once a month)

Posted by: Sidra on October 9, 2004 12:00 AM

The original IslamVeg site, meanwhile, introduced itself with the
statement that "The purpose of this site is to show what many
Muslims have long suspected: eating meat, dairy products, and
eggs conflicts with Islamic teachings of kindness to animals. Not
only that, animal industries are responsible for vast environmental pollution and destruction and also contribute to many deadly
human diseases."[25]

Compassion for Animals

The late Muslim animal rights advocate B. A. Masri notes that
"From the humanitarian point of view, it would be an ideal situation if all the world were to become vegetarian and all the animals were allowed to live their natural lives. Perhaps a time may
come, sooner or later, when this would happen. Meanwhile the
poor animals will go on having their throats slit."[26]

The late Sri Lankan Sufi teacher, M. R. Bawa Muhaiyadeen
(d. 1986), treated the matter far more categorically:

All your life you have been drinking the blood and eating
the flesh of animals without realizing what you have been

doing. You love flesh and enjoy murder. If you had any conscience or any sense of justice, if you were born as a true human being, you would think about this. God is looking at me and you. Tomorrow his truth and his justice will inquire into this. You must realize this.[27]

The Bawa enjoined his followers to be mindful of their diets and to shun meat. "My children," he writes, "we must be aware of everything we do. All young animals have love and compassion. And if we remember that every creation was young once, we will never kill another life. We will not harm or attack any living creature."[28] Respecting his teachings on non-violence to all sentient beings, the Bawa's followers have remained vegetarians.

The Bawa Muhaiyadeen Fellowship, based in Philadelphia where the Bawa taught for the last fifteen years of his life, could be considered a vegetarian Sufi sect. But are they "true" Muslims, and does their vegetarianism have anything to do with Islam? Opinions are divided on this matter. Followers of the Bawa consider themselves Sufis and Muslims, and perform the five daily prayers and other Islamic rituals (even sometimes the *hājj* to Mecca). Mainstream Sunni organizations, however, consider the BMF a heretical sect and refuse to recognize them or allow them to participate in their councils or other activities. So whether the Bawa's followers are classified as Muslims or not, it seems unlikely that their ideas on vegetarianism will have much impact on Muslim society as a whole.

Of course ethical concern for the rights of animals does not necessarily lead to vegetarianism, nor is it the only possible justification for it. Another major motivation is human health. Especially among Sufis, austerities aimed at purifying the body have sometimes entailed abstention from animal flesh. The Indian saint Shaykh Nasir al-Din Mahmud (d. 1356), known as "The Lamp of Delhi," ate plain rice or rice with lentils (a mixture we now know to be protein-complementary!), or else bread and sometimes melons and sweets.[29]

Such practices were not limited to the Indian environment. Even Hellenistically influenced Sufis have sometimes shunned

meat-eating as nourishing the "animal soul" or *nafs* (also translated as "the lower self"). The famous Sufi philosopher Muhyi
al-din ibn 'Arabi, in his *Treatise of Lights* (*Risālat al-anwār*),
admonishes the reader to "[b]e careful of your diet. It is better if
your food be nourishing but devoid of animal fat."[30] In his commentary on this passage, 'Abd al-Karim ibn Ibrahim al-Jili notes
that this is ". . . because animal fat strengthens animality, and its
principles will dominate spiritual principles."[31]

Mainstream Islam has never encouraged asceticism in the way
many Sufi traditions have. But in light of present-day scientific
perspectives on nutritional health, it is clear that Muslims can
enjoy physical as well as spiritual benefits from a vegetarian diet.
Both aspects would seem to be fully compatible with established
Islamic principles of animal rights.

Determining Lawful Foods: A Growing Challenge for Muslims

Muslims, like Jews and Hindus, are known for having certain
dietary restrictions. The Qur'an specifically forbids a number of
types of foods, which are known as *harām*. Acceptable foods, by
contrast, are categorized as *halāl*. A devout Muslim will take care
to consume only the latter and shun the former. Foods about
which there is doubt (*mashbūh* or *mashkūk*) are also to be
avoided.

On the surface of it, making the distinction between *halāl* and
harām food items would seem fairly straightforward, since the
conditions laid down in the Qur'an for food to be lawful are clear
and simple, based on verses such as those mentioned earlier.[32]
The Qur'an permits Muslims to eat the meat of any herbivorous
animal which has been properly slaughtered (that is to say, by a
Muslim, invoking the name of Allah, completely bled, et cetera),
with certain exceptions such as pigs.

Today, however, with most food being produced industrially,
it is increasingly difficult for Muslims to be certain that even these
basic conditions have been met. Even food labeled as *halāl* often
isn't, a problem that has been addressed by recent legislation in

New Jersey, Illinois, Minnesota, California, and Michigan making false labeling a crime. Still, as B. A. Masri observes:

> It is almost impossible these days for Muslims to totally avoid consuming unlawful (*harām*) things in ignorance. Even some of the items of everyday consumption, which are taken for granted as lawful (*halāl*) contain forbidden ingredients. For example, bread, cakes, biscuits, confectionery, frozen foods, dairy products, tinned fruits and vegetables, soups and a hoard of other items contain additives and preservatives extracted from meats, bones and fats of unlawful animals and are of doubtful (*mashkūk*) origin.[33]

In North America, the Islamic Food and Nutrition Council (IFANCA) exists to allay any concerns Muslims may have regarding their diet. Their website and online newsletter, as well as a print publication, *Halal Consumer* ("We Take the Doubt Out of Doubtful"), claim to speak authoritatively on which modern foods and food distributors are *halāl* and which are not, providing "shopper's guides" and lists of "reliable" food companies.[34] Their columnists repeatedly emphasize the principle that "everything is *halāl* unless specifically prohibited," but caution that "doubtful things should be avoided."

Nevertheless, the approach taken by *Halal Consumer* is generally uncritical when it comes to modern food production techniques, focusing on following the letter of the law rather than looking to what the underlying spirit (health, compassion) might have been. Biotechnology and the use of genetically-modified organisms (GMOs) are embraced, and there is no critique of factory farming or the administering of hormones and antibiotics to livestock. Readers are urged only to avoid items which may contain alcohol or pork products, and to "investigate further" some ingredients or chemical additives that may come from "*harām* animals, alcohol, or *halāl* animals slaughtered by non-Muslims."[35] Where there is the possibility of Muslims consuming even the minutest amounts of such items, the Council is meticulous; on other issues, whether pertaining to human health problems not foreseen in the Qur'an or to the welfare of animals in general, they are silent. Another *halāl* certification organization, the Muslim Consumer Group, also provides Muslims with guidance in this area, but their position as stated on a now-defunct message board is that vegetarianism is essentially un-Islamic.[36]

It is worth noting that Middle Eastern countries now import much of their meat from places such as New Zealand, and that factory farming (in which animal remains are typically fed to other animals) presents considerable difficulties in verifying whether meat is *halāl*. Especially in the West, where the disease known as Bovine Spongiform Encephalopathy (BSE, or "Mad Cow Disease") is a growing concern, some Muslims are beginning to ask questions beyond the simple matter of whether the animals they eat have been slaughtered according to *halāl* regulations.

For example, the director of the North American Halal Foundation, Mazhar Hussaini, has recently made the point that Muslims are required to eat meat that is not only *halāl* ("permissible"), but also *tayyib* (literally, "good," "all right"), which he defines as "wholesome, pure, nutritious and safe."[37] In response to this emerging concern at least one Islamic meat distributor, Dakota Halal Inc., now offers *halāl* meat from animals that have been raised on all-vegetable diets.

Among leading contemporary Muslim intellectuals, the prolific and controversial Swiss-born academic Tariq Ramadan (a grandson of Egyptian Islamist Hasan al-Banna) is rare in his refusal to be satisfied with the mere preoccupation of whether one's meat technically meets the requirements for *halāl* slaughter. "Muslims would do well not to rush into formulaic arguments on this point," he writes, adding that

> they often concentrate simply on the way an animal is slaughtered and not on the way it is treated during its life before the ritual slaughter. It must be said repeatedly that Islamic teachings on respect for animal life are clear. The way in which sheep and other animals are treated is unacceptable, and farms where care is taken to allow animals to

grow naturally and with respect are in fact more *Islamic* than is the simple application of formal rules for sacrifice.[38]

Ramadan's observation is poignant, but he chooses to bury it in a footnote in his latest book, an indication of the relatively minor importance he accords animal rights in comparison with other issues. Nor does he seem interested in pursuing his criticism on factory farming conditions, any further than the simple remark that they are "unacceptable."

Meanwhile, some recent postings to the Islamic women's internet site *Al-Muhajabah* offer a higher level of critical reflection on this topic:

> Some Muslims in the West are partly or wholly vegetarian because it's difficult for them to find *halāl* (lawfully slaughtered) meat. I fall into this category. However, Islamic vegetarianism advocates go beyond this. As I understand it, their view is that *halāl* butchers and others who provide slaughtering services get the animals from farms that do not treat the animals in accordance with Islamic rules . . . In other words, even "*halāl* meat" is not really *halāl* and Muslims should refrain from eating it.[39]

Another posting to the same site puts the issue even more succinctly:

> . . . how can the meat we eat be morally sound (a necessary condition for something to be *halāl*), when the animal has been tortured (contrary to the Prophet's (PBUH) teachings)? This meat is also impure because of the additions of unnatural growth hormones.[40]

It would seem that in the case of applying a deeper and more critical approach to the question of *halāl* meat than the jurists are doing, perhaps ordinary Muslim women are prepared to take the lead. As with the legal thinkers, however, there is little evidence so far of any cross-fertilization of ideas resulting from reading Western critical scholarship on animals. That is to say that Muslim women vegetarians do not yet seem to have begun to explore the linkages between the violence of patriarchy and that of meat-eating, as one sees for example in the work of Carol Adams.[41]

Islamic Social Justice and Animal Rights

Muhammad of Mecca was one of history's most influential social reformers. He lived at a time of social change and upheaval in western Arabia, when some families were enjoying untold wealth while others suffered in deprivation. Consequently, social justice is one of the major themes of the Qur'an.[42] Muhammad's insistent preaching against the hypocrisy of Mecca's wealthy elite was likely to have been a major factor accounting for the persecution suffered by the early Muslim community.

In most societies today, meat-eating remains by and large a privilege of the wealthy. This is a privilege which comes at a cost not only to the animals who are slaughtered for the tables of the rich, but also in the form of chronic hunger for 20 percent of the world's human population, a disproportionate number of whom are Muslims. Even while so many human beings go permanently malnourished, more than half of all land under cultivation is given over to crops destined for livestock consumption. As contemporary philosopher Peter Singer, guru of the Animal Liberation movement, puts it, "the raising of animals for food by the methods used in the industrial nations does not contribute to the solution of the hunger problem. On the contrary, it aggravates it enormously."[43]

A report from the time of the second Caliph, 'Umar, seems relevant to the contemporary situation in which the eating of meat by some is tied to the deprivation of sustenance to others:

> Yahya related to me from Malik from Yahya ibn Said that Umar ibn al-Khattab saw Jabir ibn Abdullah carrying some meat. He said, "What is this?" He said, "*Amir al-muminin* ([O] Commander of the Faithful). We desired meat and I bought some meat for a dirham." Umar said, "Does any one of you want to fill his belly apart from his neighbor or nephew? How can you overlook this *āyat*? 'You squandered your good things in this world and sought comfort in them.'"[44]

A growing body of contemporary literature asserts that Islam contains strong directives about environmental stewardship, centering on the notion that Allah has appointed humans as vicegerents (*khulafa'*) over creation.[45] This discussion has so far failed, however, to emphasize connections between issues of environmental degradation and meat-eating. Among the many other harmful effects of industrial-scale meat production are the clearing of tropical forests for grazing land, the pollution of water supplies by factory farms, and the feeding of hormones and antibiotics to livestock, which then adversely affect human consumers.

The fact remains that a few small-scale human societies – mainly pastoral groups in arid climates – are still ecologically constrained to diets based on animal products. Seyyed Hossein Nasr, in his plenary address at the international conference on Islam and Ecology held at Harvard University in May 1998, cited this reality in passing as a pretext for dismissing Islamic vegetarianism altogether. And yet what is rarely mentioned is that in today's world, for the vast majority of Muslims the eating of meat is not only unnecessary but is also directly responsible for causing grave ecological and social harm, as well as being less healthful than a balanced vegetarian regime. Given these considerations, the absence of a widespread contemporary Islamic discourse on the social benefits of vegetarianism can seem surprising.

To Kill or Not to Kill?

One issue which many Muslims connect with meat-eating is the sacrifice performed once a year on the occasion of 'Id al-Adha. On this day, Muslims traditionally slaughter an animal they can afford, from a sheep to a camel, and distribute the meat to the poor as an act of charity. All over the world the streets and gutters in Muslim neighborhoods run red with the blood of sacrificed animals.

The Qur'an provides no evidence whatsoever that God is actually pleased by this annual massacre. Nevertheless, most Muslims consider it a religious duty and perform it with enthusiasm. Abd al-Jalil Sajid, Imam of the Brighton Islamic Mission in Hove, England, states in support of this view that

> Sacrifice is symbolic of voluntary submission of the sacrificer to the will of the Almighty. It is an external symbol of the readiness of the sacrificer to lay down his own life if needed and to sacrifice all his interests and desires in the cause of Allah. Sacrifice of an animal is essential and in no way should be substituted by any other form of good deed.[46]

Nevertheless, a number of recent Muslim scholars have decried what they see as a loss of the spirit of the 'Id al-Adha sacrifice. Arguing that the purpose of sacrifice is not to make offerings to God – as in pagan religions – but rather to feed the poor, these critics point out that so many millions of animals are slaughtered during 'Id al-Adha that much of the meat actually goes to waste and is never eaten.[47]

Several decades ago an Egyptian scholar, Shaykh Farid Wagdi, called for the substitution of alms-giving for sacrificial meat, but for the most part his call has been ignored.[48] Even so, during the 1990s King Hassan of Morocco banned the 'Id al-Adha slaughter on two occasions for economic reasons, citing the well-being of poorer Muslims for whom paying for a sacrificial animal posed financial hardship. And in 2001, responding to an outbreak of foot-and-mouth disease in Europe, the Imam of the Paris mosque issued a *fatwa* to the effect that animal sacrifice on 'Id al-Adha is not required and that it might be compensated by giving a third of the price of a sheep in cash to the poor.[49]

Islamic activist Shahid 'Ali Muttaqi argues against the necessity of performing the traditional sacrifice on the occasion of 'Id al-Adha. Contrasting Islam with Judaism and Christianity, he points out that "the notion of 'vicarious atonement for sin' is nowhere to be found in the Qur'an. Neither is the idea of gaining favor by offering the life of another to God. All that is demanded as a sacrifice is one's personal willingness to submit one's ego and individual will to Allah."[50] Muttaqi concludes that the existence of animal sacrifice in Islamic custom derives from the norms and conditions of pre-Islamic Arab society, and not from Islam itself:

> Animals are mentioned in the Qur'an in relation to sacrifice only because in that time, place, and circumstance, animals were the means of survival. In those desert lands, humans were intricately tied up in the natural cycle, and as a part of that, they killed and were killed like every other species of that area. Islam offered conditions to regulate life in that time and place, ensuring the best possible treatment for all under those circumstances, while at the same time broadening people's understanding of life to include a spiritual dimension and a respect for all life as a part of a unified whole. But let us not assume for a minute that we are forever stuck in those circumstances, or that the act of eating meat, or killing an animal is what makes one a Muslim.[51]

Since, unlike in early times, most Muslims today are not constrained to eat meat for their survival, Muttaqi enjoins Muslims to "cease to do so merely for the satisfaction of ravenous cravings which are produced by nothing more than our *nafs*."[52]

Nevertheless, even if one is to accord a cultural (as opposed to strictly religious) value to practices such as the 'Īd al-Adha sacrifice, it may be noted that a number of religious traditions, including Judaism, Vedism (the predecessor to Hinduism), and others, historically developed metaphorical substitutions for blood sacrifice; it is therefore not inconceivable that such a development could occur in the future within Islam. Indeed, the opinions of Shaykh Wagdi and the Imam of Paris mentioned above foreshadow this possibility.

The Qur'an and the *sunna* have been shown to enjoin Muslims to treat animals with compassion. This is clearly reflected in the established procedure for *halāl* slaughter. It should be obvious, however, that not slaughtering the animal at all would be even more compassionate! As strong as the theme of compassion in Islam is demonstrated to be, the line allowing for "humane" killing seems arbitrarily drawn. As Oliver Goldsmith remarked in regard to certain members of eighteenth-century English society,

"They pity, and they eat the objects of their compassion."[53] Peter Singer suggests that "practically and psychologically it is impossible to be consistent in one's concern for nonhuman animals while continuing to dine on them."[54] Thus far, few Muslims seem to have drawn this connection.

It is often remarked, especially by hunters, that since the natural predators of so many animals have been suffering dramatically declining numbers, prey species are in many places proliferating beyond control, and should therefore be hunted by humans. One recent case in India concerned the nilgai, or "blue cow." With the disappearance of tigers, the nilgai population has exploded, but Hindus will not allow the species to be hunted because of its name. In desperation, some Indian Muslims have resorted to the cry, "For God's sake, let's not call it a 'blue cow.' Let's call it a 'blue bull,' and kill it!"[55]

What this sort of argument overlooks, of course, is that population imbalances such as that of the nilgai have been brought on by massive human alterations of habitats, such as those of predators like the tiger. The reasoning, then, is one of punishing the victims. Is that, one might ask, the approach of a conscientious *khalīfa*?

A longstanding argument on Western philosophy is that cruelty to animals makes it easier for the perpetrator to engage in cruelty to humans as well. To one not accustomed to the shedding of blood, even to witness the slaughter of an animal can be extremely traumatic. Those who slaughter animals must inure and desensitize themselves to the violence of their act, so that it becomes routine.

It is sometimes heard in Islamic circles that slaughtering animals for meat keeps Muslims "ready for *jihād*." As I write this (autumn 2004), the global community has repeatedly witnessed the cold-blooded execution of hostages by fanatical Muslim militants in US-occupied Iraq. These gruesome acts have been proudly videotaped by their perpetrators and distributed to media outlets for the whole world to see. The means by which the hostages are beheaded is surely significant: a sharp knife is drawn across the victim's throat, mimicking the Islamically prescribed method for slaughtering meat animals (*dhabh*).[56] Those getting their throats cut in this way are said to die "screaming like animals," which, of course, is what we humans are.

Food for Thought

Islam has a long tradition of applying rational interpretation (*ijtihād*) to the divine revelation in order to meet the needs and conditions of the present age. Factory farms did not exist in seventh-century Arabia, nor were large percentages of arable land being used for fodder crops in preference to food for humans while 20 percent of the world's population went chronically malnourished. Traditional Arab pastoralists needed animal products in order to survive, yet their practices did not result in the destruction of entire ecosystems. For the most part, the early community lacked the vast dietary alternatives available to most Muslims today, and, unlike us, they were unaware of the connections between meat-eating and heart disease, colon cancer, obesity, and other maladies.

Times have changed. But, for a contemporary Islamic legal scholar to make a case for vegetarianism, the Qur'an-based objections raised earlier in this chapter would have to be addressed. I am not a qualified legal scholar, so the following brief attempt to suggest how this task might be approached is offered only for purposes of initiating discussion. The verse cited above – "The beast of cattle is made lawful unto you" (5:1) – might be compared with other verses (16:5, 66; 40:79), where the wording is equally general. The theme common to these verses is that of deriving sustenance; in 16:66, milk is explicitly mentioned whereas 40:79 begins, "It is Allah who provided for you all manner of livestock, that you may ride on some of them and from some of them you may derive your food."

The gloss "flesh of" is often inserted into English translations of verse 5:1, being absent in the original Arabic. Moreover, the prohibition of hunting while on pilgrimage would seem to indicate that hunting is an impure act, which might best be refrained from altogether. Likewise, in interpreting the permission in 6:145, which extends even to forbidden meat "if one is driven by necessity," one might choose to generalize the condition of dire need to meat-eating in general.

A vegetarian interpretation of these and other Qur'anic verses will not be without problems. In several verses, the eating of meat is mentioned as one of the pleasures of paradise: "And we provide them with fruit and meat (*lahm*) such as they desire"; "And flesh of fowls that they desire."[57] But of course Muslims are also promised that in paradise they will drink wine, which they are to abstain from while on earth. Is one to assume that, just as heavenly wine will be non-toxic, heavenly meat will be cruelty-free?

For the time being at least, such thoughts are mere speculations. Virtually all Muslims today continue to subscribe, uncritically for the most part, to arguments which support the carnivorous status quo. Eventually, though, it is possible that Muslims committed to ethical vegetarianism could interpret the sources of their tradition to the opposite end and with equal success.

Moreover, in light of the extreme injustices connected with meat-eating in the contemporary world both toward animals and toward human beings, it is not entirely inconceivable that at some point in the future even Muslim legal scholars will find a basis in the Qur'an and *sunna* for encouraging vegetarianism. It will be up to future Islamic jurists to decide if such matters are worthy of their attention.

At the very least, one might hope to hear more in the way of Islamic critique of factory farming as being incompatible with the clearly established Islamic principles of compassion toward animals. As suggested in chapter two, there could be a basis for such a critique in the legal concept of *maslaha*, which is a ruling for the common good which is compatible with the *shari'a*, even though it is not found in it explicitly. The reality of meat production today is that it entails severe environmental degradation and inefficiently diverts food resources that could be used to nourish hungry humans instead of doomed livestock – even apart from the fact that it condemns millions of innocent creatures to a lifetime of unimaginable torture. Most Muslims, like people everywhere, support this immoral system out of ignorance. Once the facts are more widely known, it will be difficult for sincere Muslims to justify modern meat production methods on the basis of Islamic legal principles.

It cannot be denied that, since the inception of Islamic civilization fourteen centuries ago, a dietary norm of meat-eating has gone largely unquestioned by Muslims, who have interpreted the traditional sources in ways that have affirmed a carnivorous diet. But from the standpoints of human health, social justice, ecological stewardship, and compassion toward non-human creation, it can be seen that a vegetarian lifestyle may in fact be preferable for Muslims. Such a lifestyle is not incompatible with the teachings of the Islamic tradition, which could be read in ways that support vegetarianism. Whether Muslims on any significant scale will ever choose to follow such an interpretation remains a matter for speculation and observation.

7

MUSLIM ATTITUDES
TOWARDS DOGS

One area of inter-species relations in which traditional Middle Eastern attitudes differ markedly from those in Western societies is the keeping of dogs as pets. A basic hostility toward dogs among the Semitic peoples considerably pre-dates Islam: references to dogs in the Bible, the rabbinic tradition, and patristic writings are all generally negative. The most common explanation for this longstanding phenomenon is that canines were often seen as carriers of rabies and therefore best kept at a safe distance.[1]

Volunteers at Cairo's Society for the Protection of Animal Rights (SPARE) have related anecdotes about catching young boys throwing rocks at stray dogs. One boy, asked why he is doing this, replied, "Because the imam in the mosque said that dogs are impure." Another, caught trying to drown a puppy in a canal, explained, "We heard in the mosque that dogs are dirty."[2]

Though the only Qur'anic reference to an actual dog is a positive one (the Companions of the Cave story in *sūra* 18), negative attitudes towards dogs which claim to be "Islamic" are based on hadith reports. The Prophet Muhammad was apparently not a dog lover, and there are hadiths which report him as saying that angels will not enter a home where there is a dog.[3] It is said that keeping the company of a dog reduces the merit of a Muslim's good deeds.[4] The notion exists, supported by a weak hadith, that black dogs in particular are demons in canine form.[5] According to some reports, Muhammad said that a dog or a woman passing in front of a Muslim man praying would nullify his prayers (although the Prophet's favorite wife, Aisha, protested vigorously against this demeaning association).[6] Because there exist hadiths in which Muhammad recommends the killing of dogs, some Islamic jurists argued that *all* dogs should be killed, except those trained as guards or shepherds.[7] This exception follows the hadith quoted below:

> Allah's Apostle said, "Whoever keeps a dog, one *qirāt* of the reward of his good deeds is deducted daily, unless the dog is used for guarding a farm or cattle." Abu Huraira (in another narration) said from the Prophet, "unless it is used for guarding sheep or farms, or for hunting." Narrated Abu Hazim from Abu Huraira: The Prophet said, "A dog is for guarding cattle or for hunting."[8]

There is a famous hadith, mentioned in chapter one, which tells of a woman (a prostitute, in some versions) who saved a stray dog who was dying of thirst, and by this act of compassion earned forgiveness for her sins and eternal life in paradise.[9] The gist of the story seems to be that the woman had such compassion that she extended it *even* to a dog, and as Mawlana Thanvi cautions, this hadith "does not, however, recommend that one take dogs as pets. There is a world of difference between helping a dog and taking it as a pet."[10]

Even so, according to a Shi'ite hadith Muhammad forbade the torture or slow killing of even rabid dogs.[11] Since other hadiths indicate that the Prophet called for the killing of dogs in at least some cases, the meaning of this hadith would seem to be that the killing should be done quickly and mercifully and not drawn out.

Though dogs were kept by Arab nomads for hunting, guarding, and shepherding since pre-Islamic times, in most schools of Islamic law (except the Maliki) dogs are classified as ritually unclean (*najis*). This means, among other things, that a Muslim may not pray after being touched by a dog.[12] According to some schools of law, if a Muslim is touched by dog saliva, s/he must wash the "affected area" seven times before being considered pure again. There is a joke about a pious man who is rushing to the mosque after hearing the prayer call. It has been raining, and a stray dog steps in a puddle and splashes him. Realizing he has no time to return home and change, the man looks the other way and says, "God willing, it's a goat."

Like dogs, pigs are also shunned by Muslims, but their case is different in significant respects. First, the classification of pigs as unclean derives from the Qur'an[13] (and ultimately, of course, from Judaism), unlike that of dogs which derives from the hadiths. Second, since pigs tend to be kept for humans only for purposes of consumption, they have never been kept by Muslims, who cannot eat them. This means that, generally speaking, Muslims are unlikely even to encounter pigs unless they live among non-Muslims who keep them. Wild boars, on the other hand, are known in many Muslim regions, and pose a special problem since even hunting them is considered unclean. For this reason Christian hunters, if available, are generally engaged to take care of troublesome boars.[14]

Still, in light of the aversion of Muslims to pigs it is worth quoting B. A. Masri in this regard:

> . . . our rejection of pigs should be confined only to the eating of their flesh. The true Islamic spirit of animal rights demands that we should accept this animal as one of the species created for some purpose according to the Divine scheme of creation. According to the Qur'an *majīd*, Allah has not created anything but for a purpose; and surely He has not created pigs for the purpose of being hated.[15]

It is interesting that although Masri's remarks could equally be applied to dogs, he does not include dogs in his discussion.

Most dogs in the Muslim world are mangy, desperate strays, shunned and feared by almost everyone. Even Muslims who do own dogs, such as farmers who use them as guards or herders, generally will not touch them. Having a dog as a pet is extremely uncommon and is taken as a sign of Western influence. In

June 2002 Iran's formal head of state, Supreme Leader Ayatollah
Ali Khamene'i, decreed a ban on public dog-walking and even
the sale of dogs, as being "offensive to the sensitivities of
Muslims." One of the worst Arabic and Persian insults is to call
someone a "son of a dog."

On a recent trip to Iran, I was invited to visit a friend's farm.
As we pulled up to the main house, I noticed two shaggy canines
lounging by the side of the drive. "You've got dogs!" I exclaimed,
these being the first I had seen since entering the country.
"Yeahhh . . ." my friend replied ambiguously, eyeing his canines
suspiciously as if noticing them for the first time. Immediately he
bent down to pick up a fistful of stones, and threw them at the
hapless creatures, who went scampering off into the fields.
(Needless to say, I never got the chance to pet them.)

When a medieval Muslim writer titled one of his books *On
the Superiority of Dogs to Many of Those Who Wear Clothes*, his
aim was perhaps less a defense of dogs than a statement about
certain kinds of people. Likewise, frequent positive references to
dogs in Sufi literature may be largely a kind of shock-value
device. In more recent times, General Parwez Musharraf, the
US-supported President-dictator of Pakistan, has made televised
speeches while holding a small dog in his arms. Commentators
have suggested that such images are intended largely as a coded
provocation aimed at Musharraf's domestic Islamist opposition.

If the Qur'an is to be taken as the primary source for Muslim
guidance, the dog in the Companions of the Cave story (*sūra* 18)
could serve as a strong positive example. In this tale, which is
probably derived from that of the Seven Sleepers of Ephesus,
seven devout young men take refuge from their persecutors,
accompanied by their dog who guards the threshold. The
account is full of miraculous language meant to evoke the power
of God: the sleepers remain in the cave for three hundred years –
or not, for "Your Lord best knoweth what ye have tarried."
Equally blurry, however, is the relative status of the men and
their dog: "[Some] will say: They were three, and their dog the
fourth, and [some] say: Five, and their dog the sixth, guessing at
random; and [some] say: Seven, and their dog the eighth. Say

[O Muhammad]: My Lord is best aware of their number. None knoweth them save a few."[16] Some commentators have interpreted this ambiguity to mean that the dog became one of the faithful, indistinguishable in virtue from his human companions.

In another verse, however, dogs are used as a simile for the human's baser instincts: "And had We willed, we could have raised him by their means, but he clung to the earth and followed his own lust. Therefore his likeness is as the likeness of a dog; if you attack him he pants with his tongue out, and if thou leave him he pants with his tongue out."[17]

Positive references to dogs in Islamic texts tend to focus on certain qualities that are desirable, but often lacking, in humans, such as fidelity, gratitude, dutifulness, and modesty of needs. 'Ali ibn Abi Talib, the nephew and son-in-law of the Prophet Muhammad and the most important figure in Shi'i Islam, had this to say about dogs:

> Happy is the one who leads the life of a dog! For the dog has ten characteristics which everyone should possess. First, the dog has no status among creatures; second, the dog is a pauper having no worldly goods; third, the entire earth is his resting place; fourth, the dog goes hungry most of the time; fifth, the dog will not leave his master's door even after receiving a hundred lashes; sixth, he protects his master and his friend, and when someone approaches he will attack the foe and let the friend pass; seventh, he guards his master by night, never sleeping; eighth, he performs most of his duties silently; ninth, he is content with whatever his master gives him; and tenth, when he dies, he leaves no inheritance.[18]

Despite this laudatory proclamation, other references suggest that Ali's views toward dogs more closely resembled the typical Arab attitude, as when he said that "Among dogs, good is found only in the hunting and sheep dogs." Javad Nurbakhsh (b.1927), a contemporary Iranian Sufi master, prefers to see in this apparent inconsistency a lesson for mystics, namely that "knowledge and training are so important that even a trained dog is considered a respected model, being of some value as opposed to an untrained dog which is regarded as having no value."[19] Another notion, unstated by Nurbakhsh, may be the longstanding Sufi premise that without a spiritual guide an individual's latent good qualities are unlikely to realize their potential. Either way, it is clear that Ali's lessons are really about humans, not dogs, who are present only for their instrumental, pedagogical value.

One case where the qualities of dogs are lauded on their own terms is found in the well-known story of Majnun, a young man whose thwarted love for the beautiful Layla drives him to insanity and a life of lonely self-deprivation in the desert. As an outcast from human society, Majnun is perhaps uniquely sensitive to the plight of an outcast species such as the dog, for whom he seems to have a special affection. At times the dog is merely a symbol for something else, as when the sight of a dog from Layla's street reminds Majnun of his beloved. But in one passage, Majnun addresses the dog with the following words of praise:

> O you with the collar of fidelity and before whom lions have prostrated. You are better than a man in terms of fidelity and more intimate with the Way than most. If you eat once from someone's hand, a hundred stones will not make you turn your back on him. Your work is to keep watch by night, and your practice to tend the sheep by day. You make the thief lose his taste for his trade and imprison the wolf in your lion-like claws. Your bite frightens away night travelers, while [human] guards are frozen in fear. On the battlefield of the righteous, one hair of yours is equal to that of a thousand armed men. When you charge in courageously, your lion-like boldness makes an armed man less than a dog. Many who have lost their way in the dark of the night have been guided to their home by the sound of your bark.[20]

Though Majnun's elegy to dogs is touching, we should remember that he is considered in popular Muslim culture to be the very archetype of a crazy person!

The Mughal Emperor Akbar the Great was, according to his official gazetteer, a lover of dogs, as his chronicler Abu'l-Fazl writes:

> His Majesty likes this animal very much for his excellent qualities, and imports dogs from all countries. Excellent dogs come from Kabul, especially from the Hazara district. They even ornament dogs, and give them names. Dogs will attack every kind of animal, and more remarkable still, they will attack a tiger. Several also will join [together] and hunt down the enemy.[21]

Here, it is again worth noting that Akbar is not the sort of personality that most pious Muslims would take as a role model. But this passage gives some indication of the actual role of dogs in Muslim India beyond the standard prejudicial accounts.

Dogs in Muslim Literature

The famous work of al-Jahiz discussed in chapter three, The *Book of Animals*, contains a lengthy entry on dogs. He takes note of the many services which dogs render to humans, and provides many details about their special abilities, how to feed them, and how to care for them when they are ill. He relates that in pre-Islamic times the Arabs sometimes ate dogs.

In fact, al-Jahiz presents his entire seven-volume opus as a commentary on a debate over the relative merits of the dog and the rooster. He begins by outlining the dog's many defects:

> You have asked yourself what merit can be claimed by the dog, possessed as he is by a vile core, a mean nature, despised as he is and held in such low esteem. One finds in him so few qualities and so many bad sides, that all peoples are unanimous in finding him vulgar and despicable; all these traits have become proverbial, with his well-deserved reputation of being unable to raise himself to the level of impetuous attacks by wild beasts, of their aptitude for self-defense and of resisting the enemy with dignity, incapable of attaining their level of savagery and lack of pity, while at the

same time lacking the mild, peaceful character of the herbivores. The dog is incapable of knowing where his interest
lies and acting accordingly, for unlike the ferocious beasts
his temperament lacks the instinct for self-preservation
as well as their ingenuity, their survival tricks, and their
ability to recognize appropriate hiding places.[22]

Al-Jahiz attributes all of these purported shortcomings (any one
of which could be contested by anyone who actually spends time
with dogs) to the fact that the dog is "neither completely wild nor
completely domestic," but a composite of mixed traits and
natures.

Still, al-Jahiz acknowledges the importance of dogs to human
society and emphasizes their unique contributions, even going as
far as to say that "the more numerous dogs are, the more one
appreciates them."[23] He relates an anecdote in which the dog's
qualities are given as a model for those one should seek in a horse:

Muslim ibn Amr sent one of his cousins to Syria to buy him
a horse. The cousin, who was a hunter, replied, "I don't
know anything about horses." "But you know about dogs
. . ." "Of course!" "Well, all the qualities you look for in a
dog, just look for them in the horse you're going to
choose." The cousin returned with a mount such that one
comparable could not be found among the Arabs.[24]

Al-Jahiz notes a number of proverbs connected with dogs,
including the following: "Starve your dog, he will follow you;
feed your dog and he will bite you, strangle your dog and he will
only love you the more"; "Faster than a dog's tongue"; and "The
dog's bark doesn't reach the clouds."[25]

The remarkable work called *The Book of the Superiority of
Dogs to Some of Those Who Wear Clothes*, mentioned above,
appeared a few decades after al-Jahiz. The author, Abu Bakr
Muhammad ibn Khalaf ibn al-Marzuban (d. 921), was a scholar
of Iranian origin who lived near Baghdad. Ibn Marzuban
seems to have intended his book partly as an apologetic for
dogs and partly as a commentary on the decadence of humans

(his misanthropy is apparent in another work, titled *Blame of Disagreeable People*). In the tradition of much classical literature, *The Book of the Superiority of Dogs* is more a work of compilation than composition. In it, Ibn Marzuban collects numerous and varied references to dogs present in the culture of his time.

Many of Ibn Marzuban's anecdotes come from al-Jahiz. The following is a typical example:

> You should know – may God exalt you! – that a dog is more affectionate towards his master than a father towards his son or one blood brother towards another. He guards his master and protects his household, whether the master is present or absent, whether he is sleeping or awake. The dog does not shrink from this task, even if he is treated harshly. He does not let people down, even if they let him down.[26]

To the oft-cited virtues of fidelity and dutifulness, Ibn Marzuban adds mention of the dog's sincerity, offering the quote, "If a dog wags his tail at you, then you can be sure that his tail-wagging is genuine. But do not trust in the tail-wagging of people! Many's the tail-wagger who is treacherous!"[27] In one particularly salacious story (which he recounts in several variations), a dog finds his mistress in bed with his master's best friend; the dog kills the adulterous couple and replaces the faithless friend as his master's new drinking companion.[28]

Ibn Marzuban argues against those who claim the dog is ritually unclean, noting that there are favorable mentions of dogs both in the Qur'an and in certain hadiths. He cites one in which one of the Prophet Muhammad's wives even brought her dog along on the pilgrimage to Mecca to guard her baggage.[29]

On balance, Ibn Marzuban's book is more a commentary about people than it is about dogs. In fact, in citing one verse he seems to be promoting one animal by debasing another: "Hold on to your dog if you can get one, because most people have become swine!"[30]

An interesting twist on the prevalent anti-dog bias is found in *The Case of the Animals versus Man*, discussed in chapter three. During the trial preparations, the council of hunter species decides to exclude dogs because of their treacherous association with humans. The many vile traits of dogs are enumerated by the bear, who goes on to say that dogs

> . . . are so wretched, lowly, abject, beggarly, and covetous that when they see a human being, man, woman or child holding in his hand a scrap of bread, or a crumb, or a morsel, or a piece of fruit, how they crave it! How they follow him about, wag their tails, motion with their heads, and gaze up into his eyes, until one feels embarrassed and throws it to them. Then see how they run for it and snatch it swiftly, afraid that another might reach it first. All these despicable qualities are found in humans and in dogs. Thus, it was their kindred nature and character which led dogs to part with their own kind and take shelter with men, becoming allies against the hunting animals who were of their own race.[31]

Logically, the question is raised whether cats are also traitors to the animal kingdom. The bear asserts that they are, "For cats too are greedy, gluttonous, and avid for the same sorts of food and drink as are desired by dogs."

Nakhshabi's *Parrot Book*, discussed in chapter four, contains numerous references to dogs, some of them positive. In the tale of the ninth night, the parrot tells of a time when King Solomon (who, according to the Qur'an, could converse with animals) was debating whether or not to partake of the elixir of life, and consulted all the animals for their opinion, but the porcupine did not answer the King's summons. First Solomon sent the horse, but the porcupine refused to come. He then sent the dog, and this time the porcupine agreed. Solomon was perplexed at why the porcupine would refuse the request of a noble animal like the horse but accept that of the lowly dog. The porcupine, it turns out, is a bit of a philosopher:

> O King Solomon, a man like you looks at appearances. It is a pity that your judgment rests on external traits. We

thank God that our decisions are supported by inner qualities. What do you see besides the visible beauty of the horse? You should consider his inner callousness for there is no hope of finding loyalty in him. He always wants to throw his master off his back and thinks of tricks to escape from his stable. On the other hand when a piece of bread or a fragment of bone is given to a dog by anyone, even if he sees him a thousand times a day, he will wag his tail and show affection for him. It must be because of this quality in him that he is mentioned in the story of The Companions of the Cave [Qur'an 18:22]: "Their dog being the fourth." A soiled appearance may conceal a gentle heart but a sordid heart cannot be seen from the outside.[32]

The lesson here is that in cultivating the virtue of loyalty humans should take dogs as their models, as the author summarizes in the verse:

O Nakhshabi, to be faithful is a good quality
Pray God that you will always possess this excellent trait
When trustworthiness is discussed, everyone agrees that
[The horse] Rakhsh's loyalty compared to a dog's was not
    as great.[33]

Dogs in Sufi Literature

Sufi texts abound in references to dogs, as well as allusions to the "dog" of one's own baser instincts which it is the mystic's goal to overcome. The following passage from Attar is highly evocative:

You have fallen low because of this miserable dog of a *nafs* (lower self); you have become drowned in pollution. That dog of hell which you have heard about sleeps within you, and you are blissfully unaware. Whatever you feed this fire-eating dog of hell, it devours with relish. You may be sure that tomorrow this dog of a *nafs* will raise its head up out of hell as your enemy. This *nafs* is your enemy, worse than a dog; how long will you nourish this dog, O ignorant one![34]

Similar images occur in *The Conference of the Birds*, as in the following passage:

> Whoever chains this dog will find that he
> Commands the lion of eternity
> Whoever binds this dog, his sandals' dust
> Surpasses all the councils of the just.[35]

Such references, which are intended as literary devices, draw their impact from the dog's irredeemably low status in popular Muslim culture. Dogs are usually portrayed as mangy and emaciated, lurking around hungry and desperate in the streets and ready to leap at any scrap of food. Sometimes they are sent by God to test people's character. Typically, the "baseness" of the dog is used as a literary foil to describe the mystic's own self-improvement. Moreover, in many of these stories the hero's lesson is triggered by his wanton and unprovoked cruelty to a dog, such as nonchalantly picking up stones to throw at it or casually whacking it with a stick.

The casual way in which these cruel and gratuitous behaviors are mentioned suggests that the intended audience would have found such ill-treatment of dogs perfectly normal. In one story of this type, a Sufi novice strikes a stray dog with such force that the animal is crippled. When the novice's guide reprimands him for this act of wanton cruelty, he protests that "it was not my fault, but the dog's. Since he had made my clothes ritually impure, I hit him with my staff with good reason."[36]

While keeping company with dogs is said in many cases to be instructive, the instruction really comes from God, as Bayazid Bistami, a famous early Sufi known for his "ecstatic" utterances and other unorthodox behavior, acknowledges with the exclamation, "If I am not a worthy companion to a dog, how can I accompany the Eternal? Glory be to God who cultivates the finest of creation through the basest thereof!"[37]

Islamic hagiographies such as 'Attar's *Mentions of Saints* (*Tazkirāt al-awliyā*) are full of such dog references. All follow the same pattern. Virtually every well-known Sufi saint, from the "intoxicated" Bayazid to the "sober" Junayd of Baghdad, is portrayed at one time or another as demonstrating their virtuous humility by associating with, caring for, or learning from dogs, "the lowest of the low" in all creation. Ultimately, as is the case with most literary references to animals, dogs exist only in a supporting role, leading to the greater exaltation of some saintly human figure. Sa'di of Shiraz, one of the great figures in wisdom literature, notes in regard to Sufi masters that "The men of the Path did not see themselves as great. They were more exalted than the angels because they considered themselves no better than dogs."[38]

The thirteenth-century mystic Jalal al-din Rumi, who is probably the best-loved Muslim poet in the world, is no exception to the rule. A typical story has him request a huge portion of gourmet food from one of his disciples. He then disappears with the food, and the disciple follows him, only to find his master feeding the banquet to a bitch and her newborn puppies. Responding to his disciple's astonishment, Rumi explains, "This poor creature has had nothing to eat for a whole week . . . God heard her appeal and commanded me to look after her."[39] In this passage, we learn several important points about Rumi: first, that his compassion is so great that it extends "even" to dogs, and perhaps more importantly, that God speaks to him directly. About the dogs themselves, however, we learn nothing of note.

Some Modern-Day Muslim Defenders of Dogs

As Egyptian–American television producer Ahmed Tharwat noted in a recent online article, "Having a dog in an Arab/Muslim household is an exhausting proposition. Who wants to wash or take a shower every time a dog touches you or licks you?"[40] Yet as Tharwat goes on to relate, for Muslim immigrants living in the dog-loving United States, owning a canine can be a powerful means for overcoming cultural prejudice. Tharwat reports that soon after succumbing to his daughter's insistence that the family acquire a dog, "Strangers who used to skillfully avoid eye contact now wanted to engage me in warm conversation. Patriotic national hotline tippers, who are usually more concerned about

Muslim sleeper cells, now stopped me and cordially inquired about my puppy's sleeping habits, breed, and big black eyes."[41] Tharwat refers to the family dog, whom he claims to take everywhere, as his "post 9/11 homeland-security blanket," and urges all Muslim Americans to get one.

It is interesting that one of the most rigorously critical living legal thinkers in the Islamic world today, Kuwaiti-born Khaled Abou El-Fadl, has publicly admitted to being a devoted dog lover who has rescued several dogs, even including one that is black. While Abou El-Fadl has come under fire from Muslim extremists for his revisionist (and worse, textually supported!) views on gender relations, politics, and other issues, nothing has raised the ire of his fundamentalist detractors more than his love of dogs. Yet, as he explained to a reporter for the *Los Angeles Times*, "I could not understand how a creature could be considered evil when it possesses so many of the qualities that Allah asks of *us*."[42]

Because his feelings for dogs were so antithetical to the cultural values which surrounded him growing up in the Middle East, a few years ago Abou El-Fadl began combing through the classical Islamic legal sources to see whether the anti-dog views so prevalent among Muslims were supported by the texts. As a result of his research, Abou El-Fadl determined that the hadiths used to justify aversion to dogs were highly questionable and perhaps spurious. He also identified hadiths which indicate that dogs were commonly accepted in the Prophet's time, even to the point of being allowed to enter mosques.[43]

Surveying the classical legal tradition, Abou El-Fadl found that the majority of jurists rejected the killing of dogs as an unwarranted waste of life. Most allowed Muslims to own dogs for the purpose of performing services to humans, though not as pets merely to show off. (The fact that this is mentioned suggests that some Muslims in fact did so.)

For the most part the legal questions focused on whether or not dogs are ritually pure. On this issue there was disagreement among the jurists. Some argued that a dog was pure unless it carried rabies; others, that country dogs were pure while city dogs (who eat garbage) were not. Still others distinguished between domestic dogs, whose owners would presumably keep them "pure," and strays.

The conclusion which Abou El-Fadl draws from all this is that the Islamic textual tradition is ambiguous where dogs are concerned. Presumably Muslims could argue the dog question either way, yet the predominant attitude is remarkably one-sided. Abou El-Fadl notes that Muslims today tend not to be aware of the richness and complexity of their own intellectual traditions, a shortcoming he blames on the erosion of Muslim institutions through several centuries of Western colonialism.

What is clear from the dramatic revisionism of a legal scholar of Abou El-Fadl's stature, is the richness and adaptability of Islamic jurisprudence. If "even" dogs, the "lowest of the low" in Islamic tradition, can be rehabilitated through the application of time-honored juristic methods, it would seem that virtually no existing legal norm is immune from reconsideration. Long-held ethical norms may bear the weight of inertia, but they are not immutable.

CONCLUSIONS

In surveying the wide range of Muslim attitudes towards non-human animals presented in this book, several observations can be made. First, it would appear to remain undisputed that the Islamic view of the world is a hierarchical one, in which the human community occupies a higher rank than those of all other animal communities. What this means in terms of how we treat other species, on the other hand, is open to debate. Second, whereas historically it is the *'ulama'* class that have been known for engaging contentious issues in Muslim societies, at present the debate over appropriate human–animal relations seems to be most lively among Westernized lay-Muslims of the younger generation. The traditional forum for heated discussions of Islamic issues was the *madrasa*; today it is the internet.[1]

Among contemporary *'ulama'* the late B. A. Masri appears to be unique in the depth of his engagement with animal issues. His South Asian origin and his long years in the UK may have played a role in shaping his particular interpretations, which so far do not seem to have been taken up by his scholarly peers. Some of the strongest proponents of Islamic animal rights, including such figures as Rafeeque Ahmed and Shahid Ali Muttaqi, may also have been influenced by the British animal rights movement as a result of living in the UK. Other Muslims who have been outspoken on behalf of animals, such as Robert Tappan and Hakim Archuletta, are American converts. Animal rights activists in

Muslim countries, on the other hand, whether in Turkey, Egypt, Iran, or Indonesia, are often secular in outlook and draw their attitudes only secondarily, if at all, from Islam.

Despite the vast diversity of regional cultures which make up the Muslim world and the enormous potential for differing views which this diversity provides, Muslims tend to shy away from building the case for "Islamic" interpretations on any other basis than that of the Qur'an, the hadiths, and the *shari'a*. In other words, Muslim animal rights activists might not be overly forth-coming in divulging all the sources of inspiration which have led them to adopt non-mainstream positions. On the other hand, it may be worth noting that among those Muslim scholars oppos-ing vegetarianism, there is a marked preference for highly scrip-turalist interpretations of Islam. (Masri, himself a scripturalist, is an exception to this tendency.)

In terms of historical precedents, compassionate attitudes toward non-human animals are often more pronounced in the context of Sufi mysticism than in the mainstream legal tradition. In both cases, however, the tendency was to see animals primarily in terms of how they serve human interests. Concern for animals which focused on the interests of the animals themselves, while not entirely absent from pre-modern Muslim societies, was generally subdued. Despite having some basis in the scriptural tradition, any non-instrumental valuing of animals, to the extent that it may exist in Islamic thought, seems to be largely a recent development.

Whether we are speaking of historical attitudes or modern ones, it might not be too far off the mark to characterize the mainstream Muslim view as being one of "compassionate anthropocentrism," in which non-human animals are to be val-ued, cared for, protected, and acknowledged as having certain rights as well as subjective interests, needs and desires of their own. Their case is rather like that of human slaves, albeit lower in the hierarchical scheme of things.

The analogy with human slaves is an apt one, for several rea-sons. First, domestic animals and human slaves are often treated together in the Islamic legal texts. Second, the moral arguments that have been put forth in the West over the past two hundred years or so in favor of extending rights to slaves – and to women – can and have been applied to the case of animals as well. These arguments start from the premise that all justifications for setting moral boundaries are arbitrary ones.

Similarly, the rationales for denying rights to animals are precisely the ones that have been used historically to deny rights to other groups of humans: "they lack our faculty of reason," "they lack our level of intelligence," "they lack our capacity for self-control," and perhaps the all-time favorite, "they lack souls." Just as these prejudices have been successively demolished in regard to non-white, or non-property-owning, or non-male humans, scientific research has slowly but surely eliminated every imaginable qualitative distinction between our species and other animals. Differences are seen only in degree, not in kind, and if one is to deny rights on the basis of "having less," there is no quality that *some* animals don't possess in greater measure than *some* humans (as well as many qualities which other species possess in greater measure than ours). Only the issue of "having souls" remains outside the bounds of scientific study, but again, the arguments that animals lack them are precisely the same as those formerly made in the cases of women and other humans, and which (hopefully) have now been abandoned.

Nevertheless, it would seem today that traditional attitudes among Muslims toward non-human animals remain for the most part unchanged. It is possible that in the years to come new influences and emerging global concerns may bring about large-scale attitude shifts, especially as environmental protection movements raise our awareness of human dependence on non-human actors within the earth's complex ecosystems. While the number of Muslims who think in such terms today is small, it is growing, and as seen in chapters five and six, ways of conceptualizing human relations with non-human animals are emerging that are both new and relevant to contemporary needs, yet succeed in keeping within the established framework of Islamic thought.

Islamic reformers from Sayyid Ahmad Khan and Ismail Gasprinskii in the nineteenth century to Abdol-Karim Soroush and Tariq Ramadan today have criticized their fellow Muslims for being insular, ghettoized, and overly self-referential in their approach to living in the modern world. This is as true for Muslims sensitive to animal rights as it is of those striving to articulate Islamic versions of democratic governance or gender parity. To the extent that some Muslims have begun to talk seriously about the rights of non-human animals, they have done so largely without engaging or drawing upon Western animal rights discourse. While deriving a culturally relevant and internally supported ethics toward animals is surely important and necessary, it is hard to believe that such a project would not benefit from examining the arguments that Western philosophy and science have developed over the past two hundred years.

It may be imagined that sooner or later Islamic thinkers will come to grips both with the reality of a biosphere in peril and with the philosophical challenges posed by the animal rights movement. On both counts the received anthropocentric view, in Muslim societies as in Christian ones, simply has to be problematized; to refuse to do so is nothing other than moral and intellectual laziness.

As a species we have turned a collective blind eye to the bitter fruits of our own arrogance and chauvinism, and even today most of us don't genuinely appear to grasp the full weight of the conditions we have brought about on this planet. Our treatment of other animals, whether in rearing them to be used as our food, forcing them to work for us, subjecting them to scientific experiments, or depriving them of their habitats, poses many moral problems, yet for the most part we behave as if these moral problems did not exist.

The Qur'an tells us that animal communities are like human communities; it also tells us that everything in Creation praises God. If God reprimanded one of His prophets for destroying *one* community of ants that praised Him, one shudders to imagine what He thinks of our current global rampage of destruction. The best scientists alive today cannot estimate within a degree of magnitude how many species live on this earth – they guess between 1.5 and 15 million – but by studying isolated ecosystems over time they *are* able to estimate rates of species extinction, and it is clear that human activities have accelerated the natural rate by at least a factor of ten.² In other words, we are destroying natural communities at a rate never before seen in history.³

The most diverse ecosystems are found in tropical rainforests and, alongside of Brazil, those suffering the most rapid rates of habitat destruction through deforestation are Muslim-inhabited places such as Indonesia, Malaysia, and the Southern Philippines. It is easy enough to point out that foreign interests play a large role in this, but the complicity of local actors cannot be ignored.

The question must be asked, can we really be effective stewards of natural systems of which we understand so little, and when it is clear we cannot control even the outcomes of our own actions? And can we really claim to be moral beings, when the moral boundaries we arbitrarily draw around our own species community are so transparently self-serving? When will we demand of our religious traditions that they begin to probe the deeper, more difficult questions that arise when we abandon our selfishly narrow frames of reference?

Muslims have always taken for granted that the anthropocentrism (not to say human chauvinism) of Islamic tradition was adequately supported by the revealed scripture. But if the Qur'an is God's most complete revelation to humans, as Muslims believe, the fact that humans are its particular audience must be taken into account. The Qur'an addresses humans about human problems, and the tradition admits that human problems are species-specific.

What of God's revelations to other species, the existence of which the Qur'an also affirms?⁴ There must be a myriad of divine discourses aimed at the many varied aspects of creation, and it may be imagined that revelations to other species would be dramatically different from those made available to humans, given our divergent needs. Those communications might seem as irrelevant and impenetrable to us as the revelation aimed at us may be to non-humans, but it is surely arrogant to imagine that they are less important or less divine. The bottom line is that we don't know everything and we are not entirely in touch with all that is dynamic in the universe, a fact repeatedly emphasized in the Qur'an ("And God alone knows . . ."). In fact, we hardly understand ourselves or our own species! Wouldn't it be better, under the circumstances, to remain humble, and to leave the door open to a broader stage of cosmic actors than just ourselves, to allow space for the playing out of other dramas besides just our own?

The Qur'an reminds us that the earth does not belong to us, but the problem is not that we are living as if it did. No sane property owner would rip out the walls and floors of his own house merely to satisfy his craving for bonfires. Our global elites today are behaving like drunken frat-boys trashing someone else's property with no concern for the reckoning to follow. The ever-increasing masses of poor, meanwhile, are like an oversized herd of stampeding elephants driven mad by hunger and desperation, trampling everything in sight. Neither group has any vision of the consequences, and nowhere is the Islamic principle of *mīzān* (balance) being maintained. As Catholic theologian Daniel Maguire likes to point out, "If current trends continue, we will not."

Balance requires restraint, and restraint requires humility. Rich overconsumers – and this includes many Muslims – cannot go on living as if the world's resources were infinite and intended for them alone. The wealthy and privileged classes must learn to restrain their appetites for things, or one day the system will simply collapse. (The Qur'an says only that Allah provides for our sustenance, not for our insatiable greed.) The poor, likewise, must restrain their appetite to reproduce. Even in a just and equitable world, the more individuals there are competing for resources, the less there will be for each; as it is, rich humans are taking more than their share, depriving the poor of theirs, while as a species, humans are taking virtually everything on the planet, leaving less and less for non-human communities.

Humility and restraint are hardly the predominant characteristics of our species, and they may be hard qualities for us to cultivate. But we have reached a point in history when, as the Divine Book of nature seems to be telling us, our very survival may depend on our ability and willingness to take a step back. All religions teach humility as a virtue; perhaps today that is the primary lesson we need to take from them. For Muslims, an understanding of what is meant by the basic imperative of *islām* – "submission" – cannot be sought only in the interpretive texts of men. The miraculous signs (*āyāt*) that surround us provide a warning which we ignore at a cost to ourselves and to others. The earth is made up of not just one Muslim or human community but of many communities, all of them interdependent, all of them vital, and all of them worthy of consideration and respect.

To live as if one's own community did or could constitute a self-subsistent world of its own is to live in a world of fantasy and denial that is selfish, harmful, and perhaps ultimately fatal. Yet we have been living and continue to live as if it were our own community alone that mattered. Surely, in our hearts, we know better.

NOTES

INTRODUCTION: ISLAM, MUSLIMS, AND NON-HUMAN ANIMALS

1. Paul Waldau, "Religion and Other Animals: Ancient Themes, Contemporary Challenges," *Society and Animals* 8/3, special issue on Religion and Animals (2000), p. 2.
2. Peter Singer, *Animal Liberation: A New Ethics for Our Treatment of Animals* (New York: Random House, 1975). See also Tom Regan, *The Case for Animal Rights* (Berkeley: University of California Press, 1983), Bernard Rollin, *The Unheeded Cry* (New York: Oxford University Press, 1989), and Evelyn Pluhar, *Beyond Prejudice: The Moral Significance of Human and Nonhuman Animals* (Durham: Duke University Press, 1995).
3. Singer, *Animal Liberation*, p. 7.
4. Qur'an, *sūra* 14, especially verses 68–69. I have used the bilingual English–Arabic versions of both the Muhammad Asad and the older M. M. Pickthall translations, occasionally modifying the translations on the basis of the original Arabic text. Pickthall strives to be more "scriptural," using more archaic language, while Asad gives a more modern rendition, but I find that Asad tends to take more liberties with the text. In particular, Asad tends to opt for more anthropocentric interpretations in passages relating to non-human animals.
5. Zia al-din Nakhshabi, *Tales of a Parrot: The Cleveland Museum of Art's Tūtī-nāma*, trans. Muhammad A. Simsar (Cleveland: The Museum, 1978), p. 109.

6. Michel de Montaigne, "Of Cruelty," in *The Complete Works: Essays, Travel Journal, Letters*, trans. Donald M. Frame (New York: Knopf, 2003), p. 385.
7. Edward William Lane, *Manners and Customs of Modern Egyptians* (East-West Publications, 1978 [1836]), p. 286.
8. Muhammad al-Ghazali, *The Remembrance of Death and the Afterlife*, trans. T. Winter (Cambridge: Islamic Texts Society, 1989), pp. 200–1. The hadith incorporates part of the Qur'anic verse 78:40.
9. Al-Ghazali, *Remembrance of Death*, p. 201.
10. See the discussion by Marshall Hodgson in *The Venture of Islam: Conscience and History in a World Civilization, vol. 1: the Classical Age of Islam* (Chicago: University of Chicago Press, 1974), pp. 57–60.

CHAPTER I: ANIMALS IN ISLAMIC SOURCE TEXTS

1. The notion appears to derive from that of possessing life, *haya(t)* (cf. Hebrew *chayah*).
2. For the life (*al-hayawāt*) of this world is nothing but a passing delight and a play – whereas, behold, the realm of the hereafter is indeed the only life (*al-hayawān*) (29:64).
3. Qur'an 2:164; 6:38; 22:18; 24:45; 31:9–10; 42:29; 43:11–12; 45:4; and 51:49. *Dābba* also designates "the Beast" of the Apocalypse (27:82).
4. Qur'an 25:49; 36:71; 42:11; 43:12; 55:10. The term for livestock derives from *na'ama*, "to live in comfort and ease."
5. Qur'an 55:10.
6. Qur'an 2:159, 31:9–10, 42:29, 43:11–12, 45:3–4.
7. Qur'an 24:44–45.
8. Qur'an 36:36, 51:49.
9. Qur'an 27:16.
10. Qur'an 27:18.
11. Qur'an 5:60.
12. Qur'an 2:65.
13. Charles Pellat, "Hayawān," *Encyclopedia of Islam*, new edition (Leiden: Brill, 1971), 3:305.
14. Charles Pellat, "Ibil," *Encyclopedia of Islam*, new edition (Leiden: Brill, 1971), 3:666. See also Geert Jan van Gelder,

Of Dishes and Discourse: Classical Arabic Interpretations of Food (Richmond: Curzon, 2000), pp. 8–10.

15. Qur'an 5:103.
16. Muhammad Asad, *The Message of the Qur'an* (Gibraltar: Dar Al-Andalus, 1984), p. 166, n. 124.
17. Qur'an 6:138–140.
18. Qur'an 5:4.
19. Isma'il ibn 'Umar ibn Kathir, *Tafsīr al-Qur'ān al-adhīm* (Beirut: Mu'assasa al-risalat, 2000), 3:221.
20. Qur'an 22:37.
21. Qur'an 5:65; 2:61, 65.
22. Tirmidhi, 1480.
23. Qur'an 95:4.
24. Qur'an 22:65.
25. Qur'an 2:30; 6:165.
26. But see the critique of the "stewardship" definition in Jafar Sheikh Idris, "Is Man the Viceregent of God?" *Journal of Islamic Studies* 1/1 (1990): 99–110.
27. Qur'an 4:131.
28. Qur'an 55:10. Again, many Muslims see this word as applying to only humans, but the context of the verse, as well as the fact that everywhere else in the Qur'an a different word for humans is used (usually *nass*), strongly suggest the more inclusive meaning.
29. Qur'an 11:6.
30. Qur'an 2:164.
31. Qur'an 7:73.
32. Qur'an 16:79; cf. 67:19.
33. Qur'an 29:41.
34. Qur'an 16:5–8.
35. Qur'an 6:142.
36. Qur'an 6:138.
37. Qur'an 16:4.
38. Qur'an 17:44; 22:18; 24:41.
39. Qur'an 6:38.
40. Qur'an 35:24.
41. Ali ibn Ahmad ibn Hazm, *Al-Fisāl fī' l-milāl wa l-ahwa' wa n-nihāl*, 5 vols. (Cairo: Yutlab min Muhammad Ali Subayh, 1964), p. 69.

42. Qur'an 16:68.
43. Al-Hafiz B. A. Masri, *Islamic Concern for Animals* (Petersfield, UK: The Athene Trust, 1987), p. 4.
44. Qur'an 33:21.
45. The most readily usable Sunni hadith source these days is the Hadith Database compiled and maintained by the Muslim Students Association at the University of Southern California http://www.usc.edu/dept/MSA/reference/searchhadith.html. The database currently contains the entire collections of Bukhari, Muslim, and Malik, and a partial collection of Abu Dawud.
46. Abu Ja'far Muhammad b. Ya'qub b. Ishaq al-Kulayni, *Al-Kāfī*, ed. 'Ali Akbar al-Ghaffari, 8 vols. (Tehran, 1388 [1964]).
47. Muhammad ibn al-Husayn Sharif al-Razi, *Nahj al-balāgha* (Tehran, 1380 [2001]). Online English version http://www. al-islam.org/nahjul/index.htm.
48. *Muwatta Malik*, 49:10:23.
49. *Sahīh Bukhārī*, 3:39:513; cf. 10:3764–3770.
50. *Mishkāt al-masābīh*, 829.
51. *Muwatta Malik*, 54:15:38; *Mishkāt al-masābīh*, 826.
52. *Sahīh Bukhārī*, 7:67:449.
53. Muhammad Baqir al-Majlisi, *Bihār al-anwār* (Beirut: Mu'assasa al-wafa, 1983), 64:307.
54. *Sunān Abu Dawud*, 14:2536; cf. the words attributed to Imam Baqir, that "the dignity of four-legged creatures is their face" (Al-Kulayni, *Al-Kāfī*, 6:539).
55. *Sahīh Muslim*, 4:2593.
56. *Sahīh Muslim*, 3:1957, 1958.
57. *Sunān Abu Dawud*, 814, 815.
58. *Sunān Nisa'ī*, 7:206, 239.
59. *Sahīh Muslim*, 4:1215, 1381.
60. *Sahīh Muslim*, 26:5567; cf. 26:5568, 5569; *Sahīh Bukhārī*, 4:54:536; *Sunān Abu Dawud*, 41:5247.
61. *Muwatta Malik*, 20:26:89–92.
62. *Sunān Abu Dawud*, 38:4449.
63. *Sahīh Bukhārī*, 3:39:517; cf. 4:56:677.
64. See section on "Camels" (*Shotor*) in Jazayery, *Hemāyat az hayvānāt dar eslām*, pp. 60–78.
65. Muhammad ibn Muhammad al-Nu'man al-Mufid, *Al-Ikhtisās* (Beirut: Dar al-mufid, n.d.), pp. 295–6.

66. Said ibn Hibatullah al-Rawandi, *Al-kharā'ij wa'al-jarā'ih* (Qom: Mu'assassat al-imam al-mahdi, 1409 [1989]), p. 321. As Zayn al-Abidin spent much of his life in Medina, it is likely that this "picnic" was within the bounds of the protected zone (*harām*) established by Muhammad, wherein hunting was disallowed.
67. al-Rawandi, *Al-kharā'ij*, pp. 249–50.
68. Al-Kulayni, *Al-Kāfī*, 3:225.
69. Al-Kulayni, *Al-Kāfī*, 6:550.
70. Qur'an 52:22, 56:21.
71. Qur'an 5:1; see also 6:145; 16:5, 66; 40:79; and elsewhere.
72. Qur'an 5:3; see also 2:173 and 6:145.
73. Qur'an 16:115; see also 2:173 and 6:145.
74. *Sahīh Muslim*, 21:4810.
75. Al-Kulayni, *Al-Kāfī*, 6:230.
76. *Sunān* of both Tirmidhi and Ibn Maja; cited in Abduljalil Sajid, "Slaughter of Animals at Eidul Adha," http://www.mcb.org.uk/ imamjalil.html.

CHAPTER 2: ANIMALS IN ISLAMIC LAW

1. Qur'an 5:87.
2. The Shafi'i school predominates in the Middle East, except in Saudi Arabia where the Hanbali school is followed. The Maliki school prevails in North Africa and the Hanafi in Central and South Asia. Iran, being a Shi'ite country, follows the Ja'fari school.
3. 'Izz al-din ibn 'Abd al-salam al-Sulami, *Qawā'id al-ahkām fī masālih al-anām* (Damascus: Dar al-Tabba, 1992); English translation in Mawil Izzi Dien, *The Environmental Dimensions of Islam* (Cambridge: Lutterworth, 2000), pp. 45–6 (citing an earlier undated two-volume Beirut edition).
4. Jazayery, *Hemāyat az hayvānāt dar eslām*, pp. 107–9.
5. Qur'an 91:13.
6. James L., Wescoat, Jr., "The 'Right of Thirst' for Animals in Islamic Law: A Comparative Approach," *Environment and Planning D: Society and Space* 13 (1995): 638.
7. Muhammad b. Idris al-Shafi'i, *Al-Risāla fī usūl al-fiqh*, trans. Majid Khadduri (Cambridge: Islamic Texts Society, 1987 [1961]), pp. 321–4.

8. Al-Sulami, *Qawā'id al-ahkām*; translated in Izzi Dien, *Environmental Dimensions of Islam*, p. 146.
9. Yaqut, *Mu'jam al-udabā* (Cairo, 1936–38), vol. 3, pp. 175–213, cited in van Gelder, *Of Dishes and Discourse*, p. 88.
10. Izzi Dien, *Environmental Dimensions of Islam*, p. 146.
11. Qur'an 13:8, 15:21, 25:2.
12. Qur'an 7:31, 7:85.
13. I obtained official permission, after considerable haggling, to visit such a preserve near the city of Esfahan in 2001. The site had formerly served as the private hunting range of the Crown Prince; as a result of these lands being off-limits to the public, gazelle were present in large numbers. I was told that leopards too were frequently sighted, though I saw none personally. My guides carried rifles; my understanding was that these were to be used against human intruders and not against wildlife.
14. Pushpa Prasad, "Akbar and the Jains," in Irfan Habib, ed., *Akbar and His India* (Delhi: Oxford University Press, 1997): 97–108.
15. Abu'l-Fazl Allami, *Ā'īn-i Akbarī*, 3 vols. (Delhi: Oriental Books, 1977), vol. 1, p. 147.
16. Abu'l-Fazl Allami, *Ā'īn-i Akbarī*, vol. 1, p. 292.
17. Nur al-din Muhammad Jahangir, *The Jahangirnama*, trans. Wheeler M. Thackston (New York: Oxford University Press, 1999), p. 216.
18. Al-Mawardi, *Al-Ahkām al-sultaniyya wa'l-wilāyat al-diniyya*, pp. 185, 189.
19. Malik ibn Anas, *Al-Muwatta*, 676.
20. Qur'an 5:96.
21. Shafi'i, *Risāla*, p. 78. Shafi'i goes into great detail on this question later in his treatise, under the section on *ijtihād* (pp. 297–8).
22. Hesam Abdul Salam Joma, "The Earth as a Mosque," unpublished Ph.D. dissertation (University of Pennsylvania, 1991), p. 87.
23. At least this remains the standard assumption. But see the discussion in Wael Hallaq, "Was the Gate of Ijtihad Closed?," *International Journal of Middle East Studies*, 16/1 (1984), pp. 3–41.
24. Jazayery, *Hemāyat az heyvānāt dar eslām*; Mustafa Mahmud Helmy, *Islam and Environment 2-Animal Life* (Kuwait: Environment Protection Council, 1409 [1988–9]); Ashraf Ali

Thanvi, "Animal Rights in Islam," trans. A. R. Kidwai, *Journal of the Muslim League* 23/5 (1995): 38–42.

25. Kristen Stilt, personal e-mail communication, October 18, 2004.

26. *The History of Azhar* (Cairo, 1964), p. 361.

27. Mohamed Abdel Halim Omar, Final report, Conference on [the] Protection and Development of Animal Resources in Islamic Civilization and in Modern Systems, Cairo, Egypt, 28 February–1 March 2004, p. 2.

CHAPTER 3: ANIMALS IN PHILOSOPHY AND SCIENCE

1. Abu Bakr Muhammad ibn Zakariyya al-Razi, *Sīrat al-falsafīya* (Tehran: Entesharat-e Komision-e melli-ye Yunesco dar Iran, 1964).

2. The connections between all these works, together with the Pure Brethren's *The Case of the Animals versus Man* and the tales of *Kalila and Dimna*, are discussed in Shokoufeh Taghi, *The Two Wings of Wisdom: Mysticism and Philosophy in the Risālat al-tair of Ibn Sina* (Uppsala: Uppsala University Library, 2000). I thank Rob Wisnovsky for kindly providing me with a copy of Taghi's book.

3. Lenn Evan Goodman, tr., *The Case of the Animals versus Man Before the King of the Jinn* (Boston: Twayne, 1978), pp. 5–6.

4. *The Case of the Animals versus Man*, p. 56.

5. *The Case of the Animals versus Man*, p. 60.

6. Seyyed Hossein Nasr, *Science and Civilization in Islam* (Cambridge, MA: Harvard University Press, 1968), p. 71; Majid Fakhry, *A History of Islamic Philosophy*, second edition (New York: Columbia University Press, 1983), p. 173.

7. Lenn Evan Goodman, "The Ecology of the Ikhwān al-Safā'," in *The Case of the Animals versus Man*, pp. 5–6.

8. The Syrian writer al-Ma'arri evoked a similar theme in one of his works (see chapter four), but he too was considered by his contemporaries to hold marginal views.

9. They are sometimes referred to as "Seveners," since they believe Imam Ja'far's son Isma'il was the true seventh Imam and follow the subsequent line through him.

10. Muhammad ibn 'Abd al-Malik ibn Tufayl, *The History of Hayy ibn Yaqzan*, trans. Simon Ockley, rev. A. S. Fulton (London: Darf, 1986 [1708]), pp. 39–47.

11. Ibn Tufayl, *Hayy ibn Yaqzan*, p. 51.

12. Ibn Tufayl, *Hayy ibn Yaqzan*, p. 53.

13. A. S. G. Jayakar, "Introduction," in *Al-Damiri's Hayāt al-hayawān al-kubra: A Zoological Lexicon*, 2 vols. (London: Luzac, 1906–1908), vol. 1, pp. vii–viii.

14. Charles Pellat, "Al-D̲j̲ahiz," *Encyclopedia of Islam*, new edition (Leiden: Brill, 1971), 2:386.

15. Lakhdar Souami, "Présentation," in *Le cadi et la mouche: anthologie du Livre des animaux* (Paris: Sindbad, 1988), p. 13; cf. Abi Uthman Amr ibn Badr al-Jahiz, *Kitāb al-hayawān*, 7 vols. (Cairo: Matba'at Mustafa al-Babi al-Halabi, 1357–64 [1938–45]), vol. 7, p. 124; French translation, Souami, *Le cadi et la mouche*, p. 337.

16. Al-Jahiz, *Kitāb al-hayawān*, vol. 1, p. 142; Souami, *Le cadi et la mouche*, p. 207.

17. Al-Jahiz, *Kitāb al-hayawān*, vol. 6, p. 29; Souami, *Le cadi et la mouche*, p. 173.

18. Al-Jahiz, *Kitāb al-hayawān*, vol. 3, p. 362; Souami, *Le cadi et la mouche*, p. 212.

19. Al-Jahiz, *Kitāb al-hayawān*, vol. 7, p. 226; Souami, *Le cadi et la mouche*, p. 299.

20. Al-Jahiz, *Kitāb al-hayawān*, vol. 1, pp. 28–31; Souami, *Le cadi et la mouche*, pp. 88–92.

21. Al-Jahiz, *Kitāb al-hayawān*, vol. 6, pp. 16–17; Souami, *Le cadi et la mouche*, pp. 327–8.

22. Al-Jahiz, *Kitāb al-hayawān*, vol. 3, pp. 300–1; Souami, *Le cadi et la mouche*, pp. 54–5.

23. Al-Jahiz, *Kitāb al-hayawān*, vol. 1, p. 35; Souami, *Le cadi et la mouche*, p. 63.

24. Al-Jahiz, *Kitāb al-hayawān*, vol. 3, p. 345; Souami, *Le cadi et la mouche*, p. 311. This story is reminiscent of the anecdote about al-Shafi' mentioned earlier.

25. Al-Jahiz, *Kitāb al-hayawān*, vol. 4, pp. 40–1; Souami, *Le cadi et la mouche*, pp. 331–2.

26. Al-Jahiz, *Kitāb al-hayawān*, vol. 1, p. 234; Souami, *Le cadi et la mouche*, p. 333.

27. Al-Damiri, *Hayāt al-hayawān*, vol. 1, p. 2.
28. Ironically, given the reference to drymouth, al-Jahiz relates the belief that the bad breath of a dog is due to the fact that it drools a lot and that "it is a distant relative of the lion." (Al-Jahiz, *Kitāb al-hayawān*, vol. 5, p. 337; Souami, *Le cadi et la mouche*, pp. 278–9.)
29. Al-Damiri, *Hayāt al-hayawān*, vol. 1, pp. 5–7.
30. Al-Damiri, *Hayāt al-hayawān*, vol. 1, pp. 21–2.
31. Al-Damiri, *Hayāt al-hayawān*, vol. 1, pp. 22–3.
32. Unlike al-Jahiz's work, it has been translated into English, under the British *raj* in India. It is largely thanks to the British policy of commissioning translations of "representative" texts to facilitate their rule that many significant works from Persian, Sanskrit and other languages exist in English editions. Obviously, however, the selection of works translated reflects the particular interests and concerns of the European ruling class at the time.
33. Zahir al-Din Muhammad Babur, *The Baburnama*, trans. Wheeler M. Thackston (New York: Oxford University Press, 1996), pp. 334–42.
34. Abu'l-Fazl Allami, *Ā'īn-i Akbarī*, vol. 1, pp. 123–62, 223–32, 292–308 (the animals Abu'l-Fazl refers to as "noble"); vol. 3, pp. 133–6 (those he considers the "lower types").

CHAPTER 4: ANIMALS IN LITERATURE AND ART

1. Kumayt ibn Ta'laba, translated in van Gelder, *Of Dishes and Discourse*, p. 81.
2. K. A. Fariq, "An Abbasid Secretary-Poet Who Was Interested in Animals," *Islamic Culture* 24 (1950): 261–70.
3. Charles Pellat, "Muhammad b. Yasīr al-riyashī wa-ash'ārūh," *Machreq* (1955): 289–338.
4. Abu'l-'Ala al-Ma'arri, *Risālat al-sāhil wa'l-shāhij* (Cairo, 1984), pp. 123–8; passage translated in van Gelder, *Of Dishes and Discourse*, p. 12.
5. P. Smoor, "Al-Ma'arri," *Encyclopedia of Islam*, new edition (Leiden: Brill, 1971), 5: 927–35.
6. Ramsey Wood, *Kalila and Dimna* (Rochester, VT: Inner Traditions, 1986).

7. *Tales from the Thousand and One Nights*, trans. N. J. Dawood (New York: Penguin, 1973), pp. 77–8.
8. *Tales from the Thousand and One Nights*, pp. 92–105.
9. *Tales from the Thousand and One Nights*, pp. 270–4.
10. Muhammad Simsar, "Introduction," in Nakhshabi, *Tales of a Parrot*, p. xx.
11. *Tales of a Parrot*, pp. 5, 68.
12. *Tales of a Parrot*, p. 8.
13. *Tales of a Parrot*, p. 36.
14. *Tales of a Parrot*, pp. 107–11.
15. *Tales of a Parrot*, p. 127.
16. Ali S. Asani, "Oh That I Could Be a Bird and Fly, I Would Rush to the Beloved," in Paul Waldau and Kimberley Patton, eds., *A Communion of Subjects: Animals in Religion and Ethics* (New York: Columbia University Press, in press).
17. Farid al-din 'Attar, *The Conference of the Birds*, trans. Afkham Darbandi and Dick Davis (New York: Penguin, 1984), pp. 107–8.
18. Dick Davis, "Introduction," in 'Attar, *The Conference of the Birds*, p. 17.
19. Jalal al-din Rumi, *Mathnawī al-ma'anawī*, trans. R. A. Nicholson, *The Mathnawi of Jalalu'ddin Rumi*, 5 vols. (London: Luzac, 1925–40), 1:1802.
20. Asani, "Oh That I Could Be a Bird and Fly."
21. Rumi, *Mathnawī al-ma'anawī*, 1:2291–6.
22. The reference is to Qur'an 18:17–21.
23. Rumi, *Mathnawī al-ma'anawī*, 5:2008–11.
24. Rumi, *Mathnawī al-ma'anawī*, 3:3901–2.
25. Al-Damiri, *Hayāt al-hayawān*.
26. Farid al-din 'Attar, *Tazkirat al-Awliyā*, tr. Paul Losensky and Michael Sells, in Michael Sells, *Early Islamic Mysticism* (Mahwah, NJ: Paulist Press, 1996), p. 160.
27. Qushayri, cited in Emile Dermenghem, *La culte des saints dans l'Islam Maghrebin* (Paris: Gallimard, 1954), p. 100.
28. K. A. Nizami, *The Life and Times of Shaikh Farid-ud-Din Ganj-i Shakar* (Aligarh, 1955), p. 36.
29. Z. A. Desai, "Mahfuz Literature as a Source of Political, Social and Cultural History of Gujarat and Rajasthan in the 15th Century," *Journal of the Khudabakhsh Khan Oriental Library* 53 (1990): 1–64.

30. Annemarie Schimmel, *Mystical Dimensions of Islam* (Chapel Hill, North Carolina: University of North Carolina Press, 1975), pp. 348, 358.

31. Dermenghem, *La culte des saints*, pp. 97–101.

32. J. Sourdel-Thomine, "Animals in Art," *Encyclopedia of Islam*, new edition (Leiden: Brill, 1971), 3:309–10.

33. Martin Dickson and Stuart Cary Welch, *The Houghton Shahnameh* (Cambridge, MA: Harvard University Press, 1981).

34. For examples see Stuart Cary Welch, *Imperial Mughal Painting* (New York: George Braziller, 1978).

CHAPTER 5: CONTEMPORARY MUSLIM VIEWS ON
ANIMAL RIGHTS

1. Al-Haj Maulana Fazlul Karim, *Al-Hadis: An English Translation and Commentary with Vowel-Pointed Arabic Text of Mishkat-ul-Masabih*, 4 vols. (Lahore: Muhammad Ashraf, n.d.), v. 1, p. 327.

2. Abu A'la Maududi, *Towards Understanding Islam*, trans. Khurshid Ahmad (Indianapolis: Islamic Teaching Center, 1988), pp. 114–15.

3. 'Uthman 'Abd al-Rahman Llewellyn, "The Basis for a Discipline of Islamic Environmental Law," in Richard C. Foltz, Frederick M. Denny and Azizan Baharuddin, eds., *Islam and Ecology: A Bestowed Trust* (Cambridge, MA: Harvard University Press, 2003), pp. 232–3.

4. Cited on the Islam Online website, http://www.islamonline.net/english/News/2002–09/01/article25.shtml.

5. Jazayery, *Hemāyat az heyvānāt dar eslām*, p. 12.

6. Masri, *Islamic Concern for Animals*, p. vii.

7. Masri, *Islamic Concern for Animals*, p. 1. Masri published an expanded version of his original 1987 tract – originally a mere 33 pages – two years later in 1989, under the title *Animals in Islam*. The second book incorporates the original tract as Chapter One, and adds chapters dealing with general nutritional questions, vegetarianism, animal sacrifice and pigs (all from the points of view of various religions and modern science), as well as chapters on *halāl* meat and Islamic slaughter.

8. Masri, *Islamic Concern for Animals*, p. 17.

9. Masri, *Islamic Concern for Animals*, p. 2.
10. Qur'an 35:39.
11. Qur'an 95:4–5.
12. Masri, *Islamic Concern for Animals*, p. 18; cf. Idem., "Animal Experimentation: The Muslim Viewpoint," in *Animal Sacrifices: Religious Perspectives on the Use of Animals in Science*, ed. Tom Regan (Philadelphia: Temple University Press, 1986), p. 192.
13. Masri, *Islamic Concern for Animals*, p. 20.
14. Masri, *Islamic Concern for Animals*, p. 27.
15. Masri, *Islamic Concern for Animals*, p. 28.
16. Masri, *Islamic Concern for Animals*, p. 28.
17. Masri, *Islamic Concern for Animals*, p. 31.
18. Davud Aydüz goes so far as to call him "the world's greatest animal lover." (Davud Aydüz, "The Approach to the Environment Question of the Qur'an and its Contemporary Commentary the *Risale-i Nur*," paper presented at the Fourth International Symposium on Bediüzzaman Said Nursi, Istanbul, 20–22 September 1998.)
19. Bediüzzaman Said Nursi, *Latif Nükteler* (Istanbul: Sözler Yayınevi, 1988), pp. 5–11. English translation in *The Flashes Collection* (Istanbul: Sözler Publications, 1995), pp. 339–43. I am grateful to İbrahim Özdemir for alerting me to this and the following reference.
20. Nursi, *The Flashes Collection*, pp. 384–5. For a survey of cats in eastern tradition see Annemarie Schimmel, *Die Orientalische Katze* (Köln: Diederichs, 1983).
21. İbrahim Özdemir, "Bediüzzaman Said Nursi's Approach to the Environment," paper presented at the Fourth International Symposium on Bediüzzaman Said Nursi, Istanbul, 20–22 September 1998; cf. Necmeddin Şahiner, *Son Şahitler Bediüzzaman Said Nursiyi Anlatıyor* (The Last Witnesses Describe Bediüzzaman Said Nursi) (Istanbul: Yeni Asya Yayınları, 1978).
22. Nursi, *The Flashes Collection*, p. 397.
23. Quoted in Aydüz, "The Approach to the Environment Question."
24. Quoted in Aydüz, "The Approach to the Environment Question."
25. Quoted in Aydüz, "The Approach to the Environment Question."
26. Nursi, *The Flashes Collection*, pp. 654–5.

27. Pnina Werbner, "Stamping the Earth with the Name of Allah: Zikr and the Sacralizing of Space Among British Muslims," *Cultural Anthropology* 11/3 (1996), p. 320.

28. Robert Tappan, personal e-mail communication, October 15, 2004.

29. Hakim Archuletta, "The Islamic Approach to Medicine," http://www.meccacentric.com/124.html.

30. Personal e-mail communication, October 15, 2004.

31. Personal e-mail communication, October 15, 2004.

32. *Animal Rights and Ecology in Islam* (Islamic Educational Foundation, 1995).

33. See the essays in Foltz et al., eds., *Islam and Ecology*.

34. "There is no beast (*dābba*) upon the earth for which Allah does not provide" (Qur'an 11:6). A careful reading of the verse suggests that this is an inverted interpretation: it is not that God will provide for us whatever we do, but rather that whatever we have, we should remember that it comes from God. Also the word used, *dābba*, refers to non-human animals, not humans.

35. Fazlul Karim, *Al-Hadis*, v. 2, p. 177.

36. Among the best known apologists for "Islamic" science is the contemporary Iranian–American philosopher Seyyed Hossein Nasr; some representative works are *Man and Nature: the Spiritual Crisis in Modern Man* (London, 1967) and *Science and Civilization in Islam* (Cambridge, MA: Harvard University Press, 1968).

37. H. S. A. Yahya, *[The] Importance of Wildlife Conservation from [An] Islamic Perspective* (Delhi: Authors Press, 2003), p. 53.

38. Llewellyn, "The Basis for a Discipline of Islamic Environmental Law," p. 234.

39. Qur'an 13:15; 17:44; 22:18.

40. Seyyed Hossein Nasr, "Islam, the Contemporary World, and the Environmental Crisis," in Richard C. Foltz, Frederick M. Denny and Azizan Baharuddin, eds., *Islam and Ecology: A Bestowed Trust* (Cambridge, MA: Harvard University Press, 2003), p. 96.

CHAPTER 6: TOWARDS AN ISLAMIC VEGETARIANISM

1. Qur'an 5:1.

2. Qur'an 6:145.

3. Fazlul Karim, *Al-Hadis*, v. 1, pp. 327–8. It is interesting that this Muslim scholar, despite being born and raised in India where millions of Hindus not only survive on vegetarian diets but occasionally show considerable "courage and bravery," is so insistent that these things cannot be had without eating meat.

4. Ashraf Ali Thanvi, "Animal Rights in Islam," trans. A. R. Kidwai, *Journal of the Muslim League* 23/5 (1995), p. 39.

5. Zakir Naik, "Is Non-Vegetarian Food Permitted or Prohibited for a Human Being?" http://www.drzakirnaik.com/pages/lectures/index.php.

6. Izzi Dien, *The Environmental Dimensions of Islam*, p. 146.

7. Robert Tappan, personal e-mail communication, October 15, 2004.

8. http://www.IslamicConcern.com, section on "Halal Living," subheading "Fatwas on vegetarianism." Interestingly, the *fatwa*s posted by IslamicConcern came in response to questions originally asked by Shahid Ali Muttaqi, founder of the militant messianic, apocalyptic Shi'ite organization Taliyah al-Mahdi. As of early 2005, however, Muttaqi had dissociated himself from Taliyah al-Mahdi due to their "increasing extremism," and had removed his pro-vegetarian articles from their website.

9. Personal e-mail communication, October 15, 2004.

10. http://www.peta.org/news/NewsItem.asp?id=2164.

11. Margaret Smith, *The Way of the Mystics* (New York: Oxford University Press, 1978), pp. 154–162.

12. Paula Rahima Robinson, "Islam and Vegetarianism," *Meeting Point: The Newsletter of the New Muslims Project* 18 (December/Ramadan 1999), p. 3.

13. Ali Ahmad, *Cosmopolitan Orientation of the Process of International Environmental Lawmaking: An Islamic Law Genre* (Lanham, MD: University Press of America, 2001), p. 144, note 149.

14. Thankfully the article found a welcome reception in another journal, *Studies in Contemporary Islam*, more dynamic and daring perhaps in its editorial outlook but alas very poorly circulated.

15. The broader field of religious studies, at least, has begun to open up to treating animal issues as a valid topic for research, as evidenced by the establishment of a Religion and Animals

consultation within the American Academy of Religion beginning in 2003.

16. http://www.IslamicConcern.com/comments.html.

17. http://www.IslamicConcern.com/comments.html.

18. Sunny Aslam, "Vegetarian Diet on Solid Ground, Experts Say,"
    USA Today (November 28, 2001).

19. Rafeeque Ahmed, *Islam and Vegetarianism* (Bristol: VIVA,
    n.d.).

20. http://www.IslamicConcern.com/comments.html.

21. The Qur'anic verses 5:3 and 2:173 simply include blood in a list
    of forbidden items, without qualification. Most jurists, how-
    ever, have preferred to take as their proof text verse 6:145,
    which forbids "blood spilled forth," ignoring the implications
    of the broader language in the first two verses.

22. See the Organizations list at the end of this book.

23. İbrahim Tütüncüoğlu, "The Past and Current Situation
    of Vegetarianism in Turkey," *European Vegetarian Union
    News* (1998), issue 4 and (1999), issue 1: online version
    http://www.ivu.org/evu/english/news/index.html.

24. Baquer Namazi, "Environmental NGOs," *Situational Analysis
    of NGOs in Iran* (Tehran: United Nations Development Pro-
    gramme, 2000), appendix.

25. http://www.godsdirectcontact.com/vegetarian/abc/veg.htm.

26. Masri, *Animals in Islam*, p. 36.

27. M. R. Bawa Muhaiyadeen, *Come to the Secret Garden: Sufi
    Tales of Wisdom* (Philadelphia: Fellowship Press, 1985), p. 26.

28. Muhaiyadeen, *Come to the Secret Garden*, p. 28.

29. Khaliq Ahmad Nizami, *The Life and Times of Shaikh Nasir-
    u'd-din Chiragh-i-Delhi* (Delhi: Idarah-i Adabiyyat, 1991),
    p. 57, citing Sayyid Muhammad Gisu Daraz, *Jawami' al-Kalim*,
    p. 162. I am grateful to Emil Ansarov for alerting me to this and
    the following two references.

30. Muhyi al-Din ibn 'Arabi, *Risalat al-Anwar*, tr. Rabia Terri
    Harris, *Journey to the Lord of Power* (Rochester, Vermont:
    Inner Traditions International, 1989 [1981]), p. 31.

31. 'Abd al-Karim ibn Ibrahim al-Jili, *Isfar 'an risālat al-anwār*, in
    Harris, p. 81.

32. Qur'an 5:1, 5:3, and others.

33. Masri, *Animals in Islam*, p. 158.

34. http://www.ifanca.org.
35. *Halal Consumer* (Spring 2003): 34.
36. Robert Tappan, personal e-mail communication, October 25, 2004.
37. "Mad Cow: It is Time to be Organic and Natural," http://www.soundvision.com/info/halalhealthy/organicornot.asp.
38. Tariq Ramadan, *Western Muslims and the Future of Islam* (New York: Oxford, 2004), pp. 243–4, note 12.
39. "Islamic Vegetarianism," http://www.muhajabah.com/islamicblog/archives/veiled4allah/005184.php (April 19, 2003).
40. Elham Shahabat, http://www.muhajabah.com/islamicblog/archives/veiled4allah/005184.php (April 19, 2003).
41. Carol Adams, *The Sexual Politics of Meat* (New York: Continuum, 1990).
42. See for example Sayyid Qutb, *Social Justice in Islam*, trans. William Shepard (Leiden: Brill, 1996).
43. Singer, *Animal Liberation*, p. 180.
44. *Muwatta Malik*, 49.36. The Qur'anic verse is 46:20.
45. Izzi Dien, *Environmental Dimensions of Islam*; see also Akhtaruddin Ahmad, *Islam and the Environmental Crisis* (London: Ta-ha Publishers, 1997); Abou Bakr Ahmed Ba Kader et al., eds., *Islamic Principles for the Conservation of the Natural Environment* (Gland, Switzerland: International Union for the Conservation of the Natural Environment, 1983); Seyyed Hossein Nasr, *Man and Nature: The Spiritual Crisis of Modern Man* (Chicago: Kazi, 2000 [1967]); Iqtidar H. Zaidi, "On the Ethics of Man's Interaction with the Environment: An Islamic Approach," *Environmental Ethics* 3/1 (1981): 35–47; the essays in Harfiya Abdel Haleem, ed., *Islam and the Environment* (London: Ta-ha Publishers, 1998); Fazlun Khalid and Joanne O'Brien, eds., *Islam and Ecology* (New York: Cassell, 1992); and Foltz et al., eds., *Islam and Ecology*.
46. Sajid, "Slaughter of Animals at Eidul Adha."
47. Masri, *Animals in Islam*, pp. 117–19.
48. Masri, *Animals in Islam*, p. 117.
49. "French Shun Sacrifice," *Islamic Voice* 15–04/172 (April 2001/Muharram 1422).
50. Shahid 'Ali Muttaqi, "[An] Islamic Perspective Against Animal Sacrifice," http://www.islamicconcern.com/sacrifice01.asp.

51. Muttaqi, "[An] Islamic Perspective."
52. Muttaqi, "[An] Islamic Perspective."
53. Oliver Goldsmith, "The Citizen of the World," in *Collected Works,* ed. A. Friedman 5 vols. (Oxford: Clarendon Press, 1966), 2:60.
54. Singer, *Animal Liberation,* p. 172.
55. Related by Muhammad Aslam Parvaiz at the Islam and Ecology conference, Harvard University, 8 May 1998.
56. Mimicking, though not following exactly, since *dhabh* slaughter is not supposed to result in the complete removal of the animal's head.
57. Qur'an 52:22 and 56:21. Of course, likening meat to other heavenly pleasures forbidden on earth could be compatible with some, though not all, arguments for vegetarianism.

CHAPTER 7: MUSLIM ATTITUDES TOWARDS DOGS

1. Sophia Menache, "Dogs: God's Worst Enemies?" *Society and Animals* 5/1 (1997), p. 37.
2. Kristen Stilt, "How Muslims Can Wage Jihad Against 'Islamic' Cruelty," *Animal People* (May 2004), p. 6.
3. *Sahīh Muslim,* 4:174, 175.
4. Malik ibn Anas, *Muwatta,* 2:969.
5. Ahmad ibn Hanbal, *Musnad,* 5:194, 197.
6. *Sahīh Muslim,* 4:1038, 1039.
7. See for example, Fazlul Karim, *Al-Hadis,* v. 2, p. 177; also *Muwatta,* 54:54.5, 12–13; *Sahīh Muslim* 24:5246, 5248; and *Sahīh Bukhārī,* vol. 4, 54:528, 541.
8. *Sahīh Bukhārī,* 3:39:515; cf. 7:67:389, 390, 391.
9. See note 65, p. 156.
10. Thanvi, "Animal's Rights in Islam," p. 41.
11. *Nahj al-balāgha,* p. 47; cited in Jazayery, *Hemāyat az hayvānāt dar eslām,* p. 59.
12. The Hanafi school of law, more lenient than the others in many respects, does not have this restriction.
13. Qur'an 5:3.
14. This tension forms the plot of contemporary Iranian playwright Gholam-Hossein Sa'edi's play "The Stick-Wielders of Varazil," in which an Armenian Christian is called upon to save a rural village from the predations of wild boars. A similar drama,

minus the Christian hunters, occurs towards the end of Bahram Bayza'i's film *Bashu*.

15. Masri, *Animals in Islam*, p. 68.
16. Qur'an 18:22.
17. Qur'an 7:176.
18. Hafiz Hussain ibn Karbala'i, *Rawzāt al-jinān wa jannāt al-janān* (Tehran, 1965), p. 414.
19. Javad Nurbakhsh, *Dogs from a Sufi Point of View* (London: Khaniqahi-nimatullahi Publications, 1989), p. xii.
20. 'Abd al-Rahman Jami, *Haft Awrang* (Tehran, 1978), p. 875.
21. Abu'l-Fazl Allami, *Ā'īn-i Akbarī*, vol. 1, p. 301.
22. Al-Jahiz, *Kitāb al-hayawān*, vol. 1, p. 102; Souami, *Le cadi et la mouche*, p. 291.
23. Al-Jahiz, *Kitāb al-hayawān*, vol. 2, p. 178; Souami, *Le cadi et la mouche*, p. 288.
24. Al-Jahiz, *Kitāb al-hayawān*, vol. 2, p. 363; Souami, *Le cadi et la mouche*, p. 284.
25. Souami, *Le cadi et la mouche*, p. 358.
26. Muhammad ibn Khalaf ibn al-Marzuban, *The Book of the Superiority of Dogs to Many of Those Who Wear Clothes*, trans. G. R. Smith and M. A. S. Abdel Haleem (Warminster, England: Aris and Phillips, 1978), p. 8; cf. al-Jahiz, *Kitāb al-hayawān*, v. 2, p. 173.
27. Ibn Marzuban, *The Superiority of Dogs*, p. 9.
28. Ibn Marzuban, *The Superiority of Dogs*, pp. 30–31.
29. Ibn Marzuban, *The Superiority of Dogs*, p. 15.
30. Ibn Marzuban, *The Superiority of Dogs*, p. 12.
31. *The Case of the Animals versus Man*, pp. 87–8.
32. *Tales of a Parrot*, p. 72.
33. *Tales of a Parrot*, p. 72. Rakhsh was the horse of the pre-Islamic Iranian hero Rostam, known from Ferdowsi's epic the *Book of Kings* (*Shah-nameh*).
34. Farid al-din 'Attar, *Musibat-nāma* (Tehran, 1977), p. 182.
35. Attar, *Conference of the Birds*, p. 97.
36. Farid al-din 'Attar, *Elāhī-nāmeh* (Tehran, 1980), p. 46.
37. Farid al-din 'Attar, *Tazkirat al-awliyā* (Tehran, 1975), p. 172.
38. Muslih al-din Sa'di, *Bustān* (Tehran, 1977), p. 328.
39. Awhad al-din Kermani, *Manāqib* (Tehran, 1969), v. 1, p. 377.

40. Ahmed Tharwat, "Love My Dog, Love Me: The Great Arab-American Puppy Story," *Slate* (November 12, 2004), http://slate.msn.com/id/2109596.

41. Tharwat, "Love My Dog, Love Me."

42. Teresa Watanabe, "Battling Islamic Puritans," *Los Angeles Times* (January 2, 2002): A1.

43. Khalid Abou El-Fadl, "Dogs in Islam," in Bron Taylor, ed., *Encyclopedia of Religion and Nature* (New York: Continuum, 2005), pp. 498–500.

CONCLUSIONS

1. Anthropologist Robert Hefner notes in this regard that "In contrast to an age when Islamic knowledge was the monopoly of a small number of jurists, Islamic knowledge and practice today are objects of interest for growing numbers of people." (Robert W. Hefner, "Multiple Modernities: Christianity, Islam and Hinduism in a Globalizing Age," *Annual Reviews of Anthropology* 27 (1998), p. 91.) Eickelman and Piscatori refer to this transformation in the nature of Islamic contestation as "the objectification of religious knowledge" (Dale F. Eickelman and James Piscatori, *Muslim Politics* (Princeton: Princeton University Press, 1996), p. 38). Of course this phenomenon has a dark side, as websites such as those of al-Qa'eda and other such unschooled extremist organizations compete successfully with established 'ulama' for interpretive authority.

2. See Edward O. Wilson, *The Diversity of Life* (New York: Norton, 1993).

3. The scale of this catastrophe is such that scientists now say we are living through the earth's "sixth extinction event," the last one having been 65 million years ago and presumably caused by an asteroid. This time the cause is a purely terrestrial one: uncontrolled human activities. See Richard Leakey, *The Sixth Extinction: Patterns of Life and the Future of Humankind* (New York: Doubleday, 1995).

4. Qur'an 16:68.

BIBLIOGRAPHY

Abou El-Fadl, Khalid, "Dogs in Islam," in Bron Taylor, ed., *Encyclopedia of Religion and Nature* (New York: Continuum, 2005), pp. 498–500.

Abu'l-Fazl Allami, *Ā'īn-i Akbarī*, 3 vols. (Delhi: Oriental Books, 1977).

Adams, Carol, *The Sexual Politics of Meat* (New York: Continuum, 1990).

Ahmad, Ali, *Cosmopolitan Orientation of the Process of International Environmental Lawmaking: An Islamic Law Genre* (Lanham, MD: University Press of America, 2001).

Ahmed, Rafeeque, *Islam and Vegetarianism* (Bristol: VIVA, n.d.).

Animal Rights and Ecology in Islam (Islamic Educational Foundation, 1995).

"Animals' Angels in Egypt: Different Cultures, New Approaches, Common Successes," *Animals' Angels Newsletter* (January 2002), pp. 5–6.

Asad, Muhammad, *The Message of the Qur'an* (Gibraltar: Dar Al-Andalus, 1984).

Asani, Ali S., "Oh That I Could Be a Bird and Fly, I Would Rush to the Beloved," in Paul Waldau and Kimberley Patton, eds., *A Communion of Subjects: Animals in Religion and Ethics* (New York: Columbia University Press, in press).

'Attar, Farid al-din, *Tazkirat al-Awliyā*, tr. Paul Losensky and Michael Sells, in Michael Sells, *Early Islamic Mysticism* (Mahwah: Paulist Press, 1996).

——, *The Conference of the Birds*, trans. Afkham Darbandi and Dick Davis (New York: Penguin, 1984).

——, *Elāhī-nāmeh* (Tehran, 1980).

Aydüz, Davud, "The Approach to the Environment Question of the Qur'an and its Contemporary Commentary the *Risale-i Nur,*" paper presented at the Fourth International Symposium on Bediüzzaman Said Nursi, Istanbul, 20–22 September 1998.

Babur, Zahir al-Din Muhammad, *The Baburnama,* trans. Wheeler M. Thackston (New York: Oxford University Press, 1996).

Bousquet, G. H., "Ḏhabīha," *Encyclopedia of Islam,* new edition (Leiden: Brill, 1971), 2:213–14.

——, "Des animaux et de leur traitement selon le Judaisme, le Christianisme et l'Islam," *Studia Islamica* 9 (1958): 31–48.

Clarke, L., "The Universe Alive: Nature in the Philosophy of Jalal al-Din Rumi," in Richard C. Foltz, Frederick M. Denny and Azizan Baharuddin, eds., *Islam and Ecology: A Bestowed Trust* (Cambridge, MA: Harvard University Press, 2003), pp. 39–65.

al-Damiri, Muhammad ibn Musa, *Al-Damiri's Hayāt al-hayawān al-kubra: A Zoological Lexicon,* trans. A. S. G. Jayakar (London: Luzac, 1906–1908).

Dermenghem, Emile, *La culte des saints dans l'islam maghrebin* (Paris: Gallimard, 1954).

Dickson, Martin, and Stuart Cary Welch, *The Houghton Shahnameh* (Cambridge, MA: Harvard University Press, 1981).

Ebrahim, Abul Fadl Mohsen, *Organ Transplantation, Euthanasia, Cloning, and Animal Experimentation: An Islamic View* (Markfield, UK: The Islamic Foundation, n.d.).

Elwell-Sutton, L. P., "Animal Stories in Persian Literature," *Encyclopedia of Islam,* new edition (Leiden: Brill, 1971), 3:313–14.

Fadali, Moneim A., *Animal Experimentation: A Harvest of Shame* (Hidden Springs Press, 1997).

Fariq, K. A., "An Abbasid Secretary-Poet Who Was Interested in Animals," *Islamic Culture* 24 (1950): 261–70.

Fazlul Karim, Al-Haj Maulana, *Al-Hadis: An English Translation and Commentary with Vowel-Pointed Arabic Text of Mishkat-ul-Masabih,* 4 vols. (Lahore: Muhammad Ashraf, 1940).

Findly, Ellison Banks, "Jahangir's Vow of Non-Violence," *Journal of the American Oriental Society* 107/2 (1987): 245–56.

Foltz, Richard C., "'This She-camel of God is a Sign to You': Dimensions of Animals in Islamic Tradition and Muslim Culture," in Paul Waldau and Kimberley Patton, eds., *A Communion of*

Subjects: Animals in Religion and Ethics (New York: Columbia University Press, in press).
——, "Islam, Animals and Vegetarianism" in Bron Taylor, ed., *Encyclopedia of Religion and Nature* (New York: Continuum, in press).
——, "Is Vegetarianism Un-Islamic?" *Studies in Contemporary Islam* 3/1 (2001): 39–54. Reprinted in Steven Sapontzis, ed., *Food for Thought: The Debate on Vegetarianism* (Amherst, NY: Prometheus Books, 2004) pp. 209–22.
Foltz, Richard C., Frederick M. Denny and Azizan Baharuddin, eds., *Islam and Ecology: A Bestowed Trust* (Cambridge, MA: Harvard University Press, 2003).
al-Ghazali, Muhammad, *The Remembrance of Death and the Afterlife*, trans. T. Winter (Cambridge: Islamic Texts Society, 1989).
Goodman, Lenn Evan, translator, Ikhwan al-Safa (The Pure Brethren), *The Case of the Animals versus Man Before the King of the Jinn* (Boston: Twayne Publishers, 1978).
Hadith Database, Muslim Students Association, University of Southern California http://www.usc.edu/dept/MSA/reference/searchhadith.html.
Helmy, Mustafa Mahmud, *Islam and Environment 2 – Animal Life* (Kuwait: Environment Protection Council, 1409 [1988–89]).
Hodgson, Marshall, *The Venture of Islam: Conscience and History in a World Civilization, vol. 1: the Classical Age of Islam* (Chicago: University of Chicago Press, 1974).
ibn Hazm, Ali ibn Ahmad, *Al-Fisāl fī' l-milāl wa l-ahwa' wa n-nihāl*, 5 vols. (Cairo: Yutlab min Muhammad Ali Subayh, 1964).
ibn Karbala'i, Hafiz Hussain, *Rawzāt al-jinān wa jannāt al-janān* (Tehran, 1965).
ibn Kathir, Isma'il ibn 'Umar, *Tafsīr al-Qur'ān al-adhīm* (Beirut: Mu'assasa al-risalt, 2000).
ibn al-Marzuban, Muhammad ibn Khalaf, *Tafdīl al-kilāb 'ala kathīrin mimman lābisa al-thayib* (Beirut: Dar al-Tadamun, 1992); trans. G. R. Smith and M. A. S. Abdel Haleem, *The Book of the Superiority of Dogs to Many of Those Who Wear Clothes* (Warminster, England: Aris and Phillips, 1978).
ibn Tufayl, Muhammad ibn 'Abd al-Malik, *The History of Hayy ibn Yaqzān*, trans. Simon Ockley (London: Darf, 1986).

Idris, Jafar Sheikh, "Is Man the Viceregent of God?" *Journal of Islamic Studies* 1 (1990): 99–110.

Izzi Dien, Mawil Y., *The Environmental Dimensions of Islam* (Cambridge: Lutterworth, 2000).

Jahangir, Nur al-din Muhammad, *The Jahangirnama*, trans. Wheeler M. Thackston (New York: Oxford University Press, 1999).

al-Jahiz, Abi Uthman Amr ibn Badr, *Kitāb al-hayawān* (The Book of Animals), 7 vols. (Cairo: Matba'at Mustafa al-Babi al-Halabi, 1357–64 [1938–45]); abridged French translation by Lakhdar Souami, *Le cadi et la mouche: anthologie du Livre des animaux* (Paris: Sindbad, 1988).

Jazayery, Hashem Najy, *Hemāyat az heyvānāt dar eslām* (The Importance of Animals in Islam) (Qom: Dar al-saqālīn, 1379 [2000]).

Johnson-Davies, Denys, *The Island of Animals, adapted from an Arabic fable* (Austin: University of Texas Press, 1994).

——, *Animal Tales from the Arab World* (Cairo: Hoopoe Books, 1995).

Joma, Hesam Abdul Salam, "The Earth as a Mosque," unpublished Ph.D. dissertation (University of Pennsylvania, 1991).

Kayani, M. S., *Love All Creatures* (Leicester: The Islamic Foundation, 1997 [1981]).

Kopf, L., "Al-Damiri," *Encyclopedia of Islam*, new edition (Leiden: Brill, 1971), 2:107–8.

al-Kulayni, Abu Ja'far Muhammad b. Ya'qub b. Ishaq, *Al-Kāfī*, ed. 'Ali Akbar al-Ghaffari, 8 vols. (Tehran, 1388 [1964]).

Lane, Edward William, *Manners and Customs of Modern Egyptians* (East-West Publications, 1978 [1836]).

Al-Majlisi, Muhammad Baqir, *Bihār al-anwār* (Beirut: Muassasa al-wafa, 1983).

Masri, Al-Hafiz B. A., "Animal Experimentation: The Muslim Viewpoint," in *Animal Sacrifices: Religious Perspectives on the Use of Animals in Science*, ed. Tom Regan (Philadelphia: Temple University Press, 1986): 171–98.

——, *Islamic Concern for Animals* (Petersfield, Hants, England: The Athene Trust, 1987).

——, *Animals in Islam* (Petersfield, Hants, England: The Athene Trust, 1989).

——, *Creatures of God*, 27-minute video lecture (Petersfield, Hants, England: IAAPEA, n.d.).

Masri, Al-Hafiz B. A., Nadeem Haque, and Mehran Banaei, *Ecolibrium: The Islamic Perspective on Preserving Nature* (unpublished typescript).

Maududi, Abu A'la, *Towards Understanding Islam*, trans. Khurshid Ahmad (Indianapolis: Islamic Teaching Center, 1988).

Menache, Sophia, "Dogs: God's Worst Enemies?" *Society and Animals* 5/1 (1997): 23–44.

al-Mufid, Muhammad ibn Muhammad al-Nu'man, *Al-Ikhtisās* (Beirut: Dar al-mufid, n.d.).

Muhaiyadeen, M. R. Bawa, *Come to the Secret Garden: Sufi Tales of Wisdom* (Philadelphia: Fellowship Press, 1985).

Muttaqi, Shahid 'Ali, "[An] Islamic Perspective Against Animal Sacrifice," http://www.islamicconcern.com/sacrifice01.asp.

Nakhshabi, Zia al-din, *Tales of a Parrot: The Cleveland Museum of Art's Tūtī-nāma*, trans. Muhammad A. Simsar (Cleveland: The Museum, 1978).

Nasr, Seyyed Hossein, *Man and Nature: the Spiritual Crisis in Modern Man* (London, 1967).

——, *Science and Civilization in Islam* (Cambridge, MA: Harvard University Press, 1968).

Nurbakhsh, Javad, *Dogs from a Sufi Point of View* (London: Khaneqahi-Nimatullahi Publications, 1989).

Nursi, Bediuzzaman Said, *Latif Nükteler* (Istanbul: Sözler Yayinevi, 1988); English trans. in *The Flashes Collection* (Istanbul: Sözler Publications, 1995).

Özdemir, İbrahim, "Bediüzzaman Said Nursi's Approach to the Environment," paper presented at the Fourth International Symposium on Bediüzzaman Said Nursi, Istanbul, 20–22 September 1998.

Pellat, Charles, *The Life and Works of Jahiz: Translations of Selected Texts*, trans. D. M. Hawke (Berkeley: University of California Press, 1969).

——, "Al-Djahiz," *Encyclopedia of Islam*, new edition (Leiden: Brill, 1971), 2:385–7.

——, "Hayawān," *Encyclopedia of Islam*, new edition (Leiden: Brill, 1971), 3:304–9.

——, "Zoology Among the Muslims," *Encyclopedia of Islam*, new edition (Leiden: Brill, 1971), 3:311–13.

Pickthall, Muhammad Marmaduke, *The Meaning of the Glorious Qur'an* (Delhi: Taj Publishers, 1990).

Pluhar, Evelyn, *Beyond Prejudice: The Moral Significance of Human and Nonhuman Animals* (Durham: Duke University Press, 1995).

Prasad, Pushpa, "Akbar and the Jains," in Irfan Habib, ed., *Akbar and His India* (Delhi: Oxford University Press, 1997): 97–108.

Ramadan, Tariq, *Western Muslims and the Future of Islam* (New York: Oxford, 2004).

Rawandi, Said ibn Hibatullah, *Al-kharā'ij wa'al-jarā'ih* (Qom: Mu'assasat al-imam al-mahdi, 1409 [1989]).

al-Razi [Rhazes], Abu Bakr Muhammad ibn Zakariyya, *Sīrat al-falsafīya* (Tehran: Entesharat-e Komision-e melli-ye Iunesco dar Iran, 1964).

al-Razi, Muhammad ibn al-Husayn Sharif, *Nahj al-balāgha* (Tehran, 1380 [2001]). Online English version http://www. al-islam.org/nahjul/index.htm.

Regan, Tom, *The Case for Animal Rights* (Berkeley: University of California Press, 1983).

——, ed., *Animal Sacrifices: Religious Perspectives on the Use of Animals in Science* (Philadelphia: Temple University Press, 1986).

Robinson, Paula Rahima, "Islam and Vegetarianism," *Meeting Point: The Newsletter of the New Muslims Project* 18 (December/Ramadan 1999), p. 3.

Rollin, Bernard, *The Unheeded Cry* (New York: Oxford University Press, 1989).

Rumi, Jalal al-din, *Mathnawī al-ma'anawī*, trans. R. A. Nicholson, *The Mathnawi of Jalalu'ddin Rumi*, 5 vols. (London: Luzac, 1925–40).

Schimmel, Annemarie, *Mystical Dimensions of Islam* (Chapel Hill, North Carolina: University of North Carolina Press, 1975).

—— , *Die Orientalische Katze* (Köln: Diederichs, 1983).

Sells, Michael, *Early Islamic Mysticism* (Mahwah, NJ: Paulist Press, 1996).

al-Shafi'i, Muhammad ibn Idris, *Al-Risāla fī usūl al-fiqh*, trans. Majid Khadduri (Cambridge: Islamic Texts Society, 1987).

Singer, Peter, *Animal Liberation: A New Ethics for Our Treatment of Animals* (New York: Random House, 1975).

Smoor, P., "Al-Ma'arri," *Encyclopedia of Islam*, new edition (Leiden: Brill, 1971), 5: 927–35.

Sourdel-Thomine, J., "Animals in Art," *Encyclopedia of Islam*, new edition (Leiden: Brill, 1971), 3:309–11.

Stilt, Kristen, "How Muslims Can Wage Jihad Against 'Islamic' Cruelty," *Animal People* (May 2004), pp. 6–7.

Sulami, 'Izz al-din ibn 'Abd al-salam, *Qawā'id al-ahkām fī masālih al-anām* (Rules for Judgments in Cases of Living Beings) (Damascus: Dar al-Tabba, 1413 [1992]).

Taghi, Shokoufeh, *The Two Wings of Wisdom: Mysticism and Philosophy in the Risālat al-tair of Ibn Sina* (Uppsala: Uppsala University Library, 2000).

Tales from the Thousand and One Nights, trans. N. J. Dawood (New York: Penguin, 1973).

Thanvi, Ashraf Ali, "Animal Rights in Islam," trans. A. R. Kidwai, *Journal of the Muslim League* 23/5 (1995): 38–42.

van Gelder, Geert Jan, *Of Dishes and Discourse: Classical Arabic Interpretations of Food* (Richmond: Curzon, 2000).

Waldau, Paul, guest editor, special issue on Religion and Animals, *Society and Animals* 8/3 (2000).

Waldau, Paul and Kimberley Patton, eds., *A Communion of Subjects: Animals in Religion and Ethics* (New York: Columbia University Press, in press).

Walters, Kerry and Lisa Portmess, eds., *Religious Vegetarianism* (Albany: SUNY Press, 2001).

Welch, Stuart Cary, *Imperial Mughal Painting* (New York: George Braziller, 1978).

Werbner, Pnina, "Stamping the Earth with the Name of Allah: Zikr and the Sacralizing of Space Among British Muslims," *Cultural Anthropology* 11/3 (1996): 309–38.

Wescoat, James L., Jr, "The 'Right of Thirst' for Animals in Islamic Law: A Comparative Approach," *Environment and Planning D: Society and Space* 13 (1995): 637–54.

Wood, Ramsey, *Kalila and Dimna* (Rochester, VT: Inner Traditions, 1986).

Yahya, H. S. A., *[The] Importance of Wildlife Conservation From [An] Islamic Perspective* (Delhi: Authors Press, 2003).

ORGANIZATIONS

Association Française et Internationale de Protection Animale
Av. Hassan II – Imm. Eddihi, 1er Étage, N° 10/11
Agadir 80 000
Morocco
tel.: 212 48 828 936
fax: 212 48 828 937

Ateş Hirsizi
Dostlukyurdu Sok. Selimbey
Apt. No. 8, Cemberlitas
34000 Istanbul
Turkey
tel.: 90 (212) 5182 562
e-mail: mexpe@hotmail.com

Bahrain SPCA
P.O. Box 26666
Manama
Bahrain
tel.: 973 593 479, 729 408

Fethiye Hayvan Dostlari Derne (Friends of Animals Association)
Degirmenbasi Mevkii,Orman Deposu Karsisi
Fethiye, Mugla
Turkey

tel.: 90 (252) 613 5825
e-mail: ragnelli@superonline.com

Free the Animals (FETA)
Jl. Gegerkalong Hilir
Bandung 40153
Indonesia
tel.: (022) 2012833
e-mail: feta@feta-id.tk
website: http://www.f-t-a.cjb.net

The Humane Center for Animal Welfare
P.O. Box 142624
Amman 118-44
Jordan
tel.: 962 6 572 86 56
fax: 962 6 571 27 54
e-mail: info@hcaw-jordan.org
website: http://www.hcaw-jordan.org

The Indonesian Vegan Society
Jl. Widosari II/9
Semarang, Jawa Tengah 50135
Indonesia
tel.: 517131
e-mail: info@i-v-s.org
website: http://www.i-v-s.org

Iranian Society for the Protection of Animals
    (Anjoman-e hemayat az hayvanat)
c/o Javid Al-e Davood
P.O. Box 14185-746
Tehran
Iran
tel.: 98-21-6435933
e-mail: webmaster@iranspca.com
website: http://www.iranspca.com

Islamic Concern for Animals
e-mail: info@islamicconcern.com
website: http://www.islamicconcern.com
Malaysian National Animal Welfare Foundation
Wisma Medivet, 8, Jalan Tun Razak
50400 Kuala Lumpur
Malaysia
tel.: 60 (3) 4043 5113, 4043 2420
fax.: 60 (3) 4041 3660
e-mail: mnawforg@mnawf.org.my
website: http://www.mnawf.org.my

Muslim Vegan/Vegetarian Society
c/o Rafeeque Ahmed
59 Brey Towers
136 Adelaide Road
London NW3 3JU
United Kingdom

Pakistan Animal Lovers Society (PALS)
Flat 302, Batool Plaza
Karachi 74200
Pakistan
tel.: 92 (21) 2621134
e-mail: sohail302@hotmail.com

Pro Animals Group
c/o Nabil Ziad Emad
P.O. Box 2937
Damascus
Syria
tel.: 963 (11) 671 8390
e-mail: krimid@scs-net.org

Sana and Shafa Vegetarians' Association
Majid Jalilvand Hossein and Gheysari Araghi
18, Mokhaberat
South Ekhtiyarieh

Kolahdouz, Passdaran
Tehran
Iran

La Société Protectrice des Animaux et de la Nature (SPANA)
41, Résidence Zohra
Harhoura 12 000
Temara
Morocco
tel.: 212 (37) 74 72 09, 74 74 93
e-mail: spana@spana.org.ma
website: http://www.spana.org.ma

The Society for the Protection of Animal Rights in Egypt
16 Taha Hussein
Zamalek, Cairo
Egypt
tel.: (2012) 316 2912
e-mail: spare@sparealife.org
website: http://sparealife.org

Union Marocaine pour la Protection des Animaux
78, rue Colbert
Casablanca
Morocco
tel.: 212 263 740, 316 279

Voice Against Violence/Animal International Rights
133 Pakiza Lodge, Lodhi Colony
Multan
Pakistan
tel.: 92 (61) 221 659
e-mail: jbasheer@mul.paknet.com.pk

INDEX